SHOULD WE CONSENT TO BE GOVERNED?

A Short Introduction to Political Philosophy

Stephen Nathanson

Northeastern University

Wadsworth Publishing Company
Belmont, California
A Division of Wadsworth, Inc.

Philosophy Editor: Kenneth King

Editorial Assistant: Cynthia Campbell

Managing Designer: Ann Butler

Print Buyer: Barbara Britton

Cover and Text Designer: Paula Shuhert

Copy Editor: Dave Cole

Signing Representative: John Moroney

Compositor: Scratchgravel, Auburn, Washington

Printer: Malloy Lithographing

1 2 3 4 5 6 7 8 9 10—96 95 94 93 92

Library of Congress Cataloging-in-Publication Data

Nathanson, Stephen, 1943–
    Should we consent to be governed? : a short introduction to
political philosophy / Stephen Nathanson.
        p.   cm.
    Includes bibliographical references and index.
    ISBN 0-534-16746-2 (paperback)
    1. Legitimacy of governments. 2. Consensus (Social sciences)
3. Government, Resistance to. I. Title.
JC328.5.N38 1992
320'.01'1–dc20   91-19281

FOR MY CHILDREN,

Michael and Sarah

CONTENTS

PREFACE

In this book, I try to provide an introduction to political philosophy that is brief, informative, and interesting. I do this by focusing on a single problem that is relevant to everyone—the problem of developing a personal outlook toward government and political life.

The book is not a survey of the whole field of political philosophy. Nor does it survey a large number of the classical or contemporary authors. Instead, it focuses on the question, how should we think and feel about government institutions? The effort to answer this question leads to a consideration of four basic political outlooks: super patriotism, political cynicism, anarchism, and critical citizenship. It also leads to an examination of some important thinkers, including Socrates, Hobbes, Lenin, and Martin Luther King, Jr. In the course of looking for an answer to the book's central problem, readers will gain an acquaintance with some central issues, some important points of view, and some significant thinkers. Most importantly, they will be presented with arguments for and against a variety of positions. My hope is that by wrestling with the positions discussed and following the debate about them, readers will be helped toward solving the main problem of the book for themselves.

The central subject of the book is the relationship of each of us as individuals to the political system under which we live. That is why I have called it *Should We Consent To Be Governed?* I first began thinking about these issues when I was a teenager. I have come back to them many times, in part because changes in the world and changes in me personally have made certain answers look more or less attractive at different times. Like everyone else, I would like to think that time has made me wiser and that my current views are an improvement on ones I used to have.

Of course, the passage of time by itself does not bring wisdom. Since I have had the good fortune to be a teacher and philosopher by profession, however, I have been able to return again and again to these issues, to read and reread works that deal with them, and to discuss them with many students and colleagues. Over time, things that used to be confusing have become clearer, and this has made it possible for me to write this book. I hope that the book will be useful and interesting to students and others who are trying to find their way to a sense of where they stand on questions about government, political legitimacy, and the obligation to obey the law.

My biggest debts in connection with this work are to Northeastern University for the opportunity to teach courses in political philosophy and to the many students who have taken these courses. The students who took my Social and Political Philosophy course in the winter quarter 1989 were especially helpful in giving me their reactions to an earlier version of this book. In addition, I received very helpful criticisms of earlier drafts from my friends and fellow philosophers, Nelson Lande and John Troyer. I thank them for their insights and their encouragement. Thanks, too, to Ken King, editor at Wadsworth; to Harvey Cotton, Bill DeAngelis, Margaret Paternek, and Deborah Welsh for their responses to the book; and to the manuscript reviewers: Joseph M. Hazlett, II, University of Mississippi; Lawrence J. R. Herson, Ohio State University; and Kerry Walters, Gettysburg College.

Finally, thanks to my wife, Linda, and to my children, Michael and Sarah, for continuing to sustain me in the most important ways. I dedicate this book to Michael and Sarah in the hope that they will both benefit from and contribute to a more just and peaceful world.

SHOULD WE CONSENT TO BE GOVERNED?

Introduction

ALL OF US ARE CAUGHT UP IN THE WORLD OF POLITICS AND government. It is no exaggeration to say that the invention and construction of vast numbers of nuclear weapons have made the lives of everyone on earth dependent on the actions and decisions of a small number of political leaders. Likewise, through laws and policies that deal with virtually all areas of public and private life, governments affect the choices we make and the extent to which we can act to achieve our personal goals. Even people with no knowledge or interest in political issues are affected by political institutions. Politics and its effects are inescapable.

Describing our situation in this way makes politics and government sound rather bleak. Many people, however, see political institutions as among the highest achievements of human beings. They think that it is important and valuable to be interested and involved in political activities. Some see political participation as a good thing that should be encouraged, while others see it as a moral duty. So, for example, when relatively few people vote in elections, we frequently hear that this is very bad, that it is deplorable that people don't care enough about politics to vote for candidates for office.

Even though the effects of political decisions and institutions are inescapable, people do have a choice about their personal involvement in politics. We have a choice about the ways we think and feel about political institutions and the ways in which we involve ourselves with them. Thinking about these personal choices may lead us to the kinds of reflections that make up political philosophy. If we want to know how we ought to relate to governments and politics, we need to think about our personal values, but we also need to think about governments and what they stand for.

Here, as elsewhere, philosophical thought begins with personal concerns: What should you or I do, think, or feel about governments? From these personal concerns, it moves quickly to broader, more general questions: What is the nature of governments? What makes a government worthy of a person's allegiance and support?

These questions are neither new nor easy to answer. Moreover, while they are abstract questions, they are neither trivial nor purely academic. Their importance is indicated by the fact that many ordinary people believe that citizens have a duty to risk their lives for their country, and in fact many people have both killed and been killed when their governments have called on them to go to war. Even in peaceful times, all governments require some sacrifices—in the form of taxation—by their citizens. Indeed, government officials have extraordinary powers: They can send us to fight in wars, take our money, and confine us in prisons. And, if we disagree with their decisions and choices, they can back them up with the power of police forces and armies.

On the other hand, governments can make us secure in our homes, defend us against enemies and criminals, educate us, and provide us with food, shelter, and medical care in times of need. Given the extensive and diverse powers of governments and their impact on our lives, it is not surprising that they inspire conflicting feelings, ranging from devout patriotism and love of country to cynicism and hostility, from "My country, right or wrong" to "Don't tread on me."

Another fact that leads people to reflect on their relationship to government is that governments claim to act in the name of their citizens. In this way, they implicate us in their actions and make us feel responsible for them. If my government engages in worthwhile activities, using my tax money and presenting itself to the world as my representative, then I may take pride in its actions. However, if my government, acting in my name and using funds that I provide, acts in harmful, destructive, and immoral ways, then I may feel ashamed of my involvement with it. Even though you and I do not choose the policies of our government, as citizens we may feel responsible for them.

What, then, should be our attitude toward our own government? In order to answer this question, we need to know at least two sorts of things: First, what are the standards for judging governments? Second, what are the facts about the particular government under which we live?

Since this book is a work of political philosophy, it will focus on the first, more general question. I want to investigate how we should think about governments in general, and when we have worked this out, then people in different countries and living at different times may be able to use our general answer to help guide their thinking about their own particular country. My hope is that the arguments and ideas in this book will be helpful to people who want to form a clearer idea about their own duties and responsibilities as citizens and as human beings.

In spite of the fact, then, that we are inescapably enmeshed in the political realm, we can still make choices about the attitude we take toward government and the kind of involvement with it that we think is best. There are, in fact, many possible choices. We can be conscientious citizens who support our government, hostile rebels who seek to overturn it, apathetic individuals who ignore politics, detached cynics who condemn politics, anarchists who think all governments are illegitimate, or utopians who strive for some perfect form of government and society. There are many possible attitudes and relationships available to us. Given the possibility of choice, the many alternatives, and the importance of the issues, we need to consider these alternatives and see which of them is best.

My own thinking about these questions has led me to identify four basic outlooks toward government. I call these super patriotism, political cynicism, anarchism, and critical citizenship. In Chapter 1, I describe each of these views, focusing particularly on what each one says about two related questions: First, is government power legitimate? And second, do citizens have a moral obligation to obey the laws that governments lay down? In the subsequent chapters, I describe these views more fully and formulate some of the reasons why someone might find them plausible and attractive. Finally, I consider arguments against each view and try to arrive at a judgment about how successfully it answers our basic questions about the relationship between citizens and governments.

As will be evident, I have my own opinions about these views, and I do not try to hide my own conclusions. Nonetheless, I try both to give each view a fair hearing and to present my arguments clearly enough so that readers of this book will be in a position to understand the positions I take and to draw their own conclusions.

Four Political Outlooks

IN TRYING TO FIGURE OUT WHAT OUR OWN ATTITUDES TOWARD government and politics ought to be, it will be helpful to begin by looking at a variety of positions that have been expressed by people who have thought and written about politics. In this chapter, I will describe four different attitudes toward the state. While I will focus on the expression of these views by writers and thinkers, each attitude is related to views that are held and expressed by ordinary people. These four views may not exhaust the whole range of political attitudes, but they will give us a better idea of what the basic possibilities are. Examining them will help us to figure out what our own attitudes ought to be.

Socrates and Super Patriotism

I want to begin by describing a view that the Greek philosopher Plato developed in a brief but powerful dialogue called the *Crito*. I begin here both because this work is one of the earliest discussions of our problem and because it expresses a strong view about citizenship in a very vivid way.

In this work, Plato describes a conversation between Socrates and his friend Crito. Socrates has been convicted by the Athenian court of preaching false doctrines about the gods and corrupting the minds of the youth. He has been sentenced to die and is awaiting his execution in an Athenian jail. As his execution date approaches, Crito proposes that Socrates save his own life by escaping. Crito assures Socrates that he can bribe the right people and help Socrates escape to safety in another part of Greece. Socrates refuses Crito's offer, insisting that he has a moral duty to remain in jail and accept his punishment.

While the story of Socrates is familiar to many, it is important to see how extreme and shocking Socrates' view is. If Socrates were guilty and knew it, then it would still be extraordinary for him to reject the chance to save his life by escaping. Nonetheless, he might believe that he actually deserved the punishment he was to receive. Socrates, however, believes that he is innocent of the charges that have been brought against him. He believes that he committed no crime and should not have been convicted. So not only is he agreeing to accept a harsh punishment that he could avoid, he is also agreeing to die for a crime he did not commit. He is willing to accept the judgment of the law in spite of his innocence and the high price—life itself—that obedience will cost him.

This is why I call Socrates a super patriot. He is willing to sacrifice his life in order to uphold what he takes to be his duty to obey the laws of Athens. He feels such extreme respect and reverence toward the state that he is willing to obey the laws and judgments of the state, even when those judgments are mistaken.

We can see, then, that Socrates takes his relationship to the state very seriously and sees it in a very positive light. He thinks he has a strong duty to be a good citizen. Moreover, he thinks that being a good citizen requires him to obey the law, even when the law is wrong (as it is about his guilt) and even when obeying the law requires a great sacrifice by the citizen (in Socrates' case, the sacrifice of his life).

For the sake of historical accuracy, I should note that Socrates appears to express a different view in the speech he made earlier to the Athenian jury. According to Plato's account in the *Apology*, Socrates told the jurors that if they allowed him to remain in Athens on the condition that he cease discussing philosophy, he would disobey this order. So in the *Apology* he seems to set limits to the laws he would obey and seems to reserve the right to place his own judgment about what to do over the judgment of the state. This provides us with a rather different model of the relationship between citizens and the state, one that I will discuss later when we consider critical citizenship.

In this book, my main concern is not with what Socrates actually believed or with his overall political philosophy. Because the kind of super patriotism that is expressed in the *Crito* is an important political outlook and because it is so well expressed in this dialogue, I am going to consider Socrates' views only as he expresses them in the *Crito*. I will interpret them as the expression of a complete view about the duties of citizens, while recognizing that this view may not coincide with all of Socrates' opinions about political obligation and the state.

In the *Crito*, Socrates argues strongly against the sort of independent individual judgment that he seems to exercise in the *Apology*. Thus, in the *Crito* Socrates imagines the laws speaking to him and saying, "Do you imagine that a state can subsist and not be overthrown, in which the decisions of law have no power, but are set aside and overthrown by individuals?"[1] In other words, if individuals can always overrule the laws of the state when they disagree with them, then the laws of the state have no real force. If the laws are to have any force, then individuals must obey the laws, even if they disagree with them.

We can get some sense of the extreme reverence for the state that Socrates thought was appropriate for citizens if we look further at the speech that Socrates imagines the laws might make to him. The laws say:

> [S]ince you were brought into the world and nurtured and educated by us, can you deny . . . that you are our child and slave, as your fathers were before you? And if this is true, you are not on equal terms with us; nor can you think that you have a right to do to us what we are doing to you. . . . Has a philosopher like you failed to discover that our country is more to be valued . . . than mother or father or any ancestor and more to be regarded in the eyes of the gods and men of understanding? . . . [W]hether in battle or in a court of law, or in any other place, [a person] must do what his city and country order him; or else he must change their view of what is just. . . .[2]

Here we have a powerful statement of the idea that the state is much more important than a single individual and that individuals must be prepared to give their lives for their country, whether in battle or in obedience to the judgment of a court, even when they believe that the government is mistaken in its judgments and decisions. It is because of the high degree of dedication to the state that is present in this view that I call it super patriotism.

Thrasymachus and Political Cynicism

A political cynic is a person who believes that governments are merely tools for serving the interests of those with power. People in government may claim to act for the common good, but in fact they are only concerned with their own power and well-being. They do not care about citizens or the well-being of society as a whole. For this reason, one would be a fool to revere the state or believe that one had a moral obligation to obey the law.

We tend to think that such cynical attitudes are peculiarly modern, that people in the past revered tradition and always treated rulers with respect. This is an illusory view of the past, however. In fact, we can find a powerful expression of political cynicism in Thrasymachus, a character in Plato's most famous dialogue, *The Republic*.

The Republic begins with Socrates and his friends discussing the question, what is justice? Since justice is a term with positive connotations, it is not surprising that in their discussion Socrates and his friends assume that justice is a good thing. They take it for granted that it is good for people to behave justly. Thrasymachus bursts into this conversation and, with great contempt for Socrates, expresses the view that "'just' or 'right' means nothing but what is to the interest of the stronger party."[3]

In explaining this view, Thrasymachus describes the way he thinks things really work:

[I]n every case the laws are made by the ruling party in their own interest. . . . By making these laws they define as "right" for their subjects whatever is for their own [i.e., the rulers'] interest, and they call anyone who breaks them a "wrongdoer" and punish him accordingly.[4]

Even the use of the terms *justice* and *injustice* is tailored to the needs of those in power. They call those actions that hinder them "unjust" and praise actions that support their own interests by calling them "just." In this way, they get people to believe that it is good to promote the interests of the rulers.

Thrasymachus draws an analogy between the government and a shepherd. Watching the shepherd giving his sheep good food and tending to their needs, a person might think that the shepherd actually cares about the sheep for their own sake. In fact, however, he is feeding and caring for them only because he wants to prepare them for sale or for slaughter. Only a simple-minded person would think that shepherds actually care about their flocks or rulers about their subjects. The stronger, Thrasymachus says, rules "at the cost of the subject who obeys . . . asserting its authority over those innocents who are called just, so that they minister solely to their master's advantage and happiness, and not in the least degree to their own."[5]

Suppose that Thrasymachus is correct. What attitude would it be appropriate for citizens to take toward their governments? Since, according to cynics, the rulers are out for themselves and do not care about the citizens, then it makes no sense for citizens to feel obligated toward the state. Perhaps they will pay taxes and obey the laws, but they will only do so in deference to the strength of the rulers. They will obey because if they do not, then they will be punished. If it is possible, however, for them to violate the laws without being caught or punished, then they will disobey them without hesitation.

From this perspective, the super patriotism of Socrates is utterly ridiculous. Socrates treats the state with great respect and high regard, while those who rule do not care about or respect him at all.

All of us have probably heard the cynical view expressed at one time or another. We've heard it said that politicians are all crooks or are only out for themselves. This common charge is both echoed and systematized in Marxist thinking. In *State and Revolution,* Lenin wrote: "According to Marx, the state is an organ of class *domination,* an organ of *oppression* of one class by another; its aim is the creation of 'order' which legalizes and perpetuates this oppression. . . ."[6]

One might think that this cynical description would not apply to governments that permit the election of rulers by democratic means. Lenin, however, dismisses the significance of elections by noting that in a "capitalist democracy . . . the oppressed were allowed, once every few years, to decide which particular representatives of the oppressing class should be in parliament to represent and repress them!"[7]

Like other cynics, Lenin claims to see through the illusions of legitimacy, and having this attitude, he refuses to play the game. Like Thrasymachus, he refuses to give any special status to the needs or interests of the state as they are expressed by its rulers. (There is more to Lenin's view, as we shall see in Chapter 3.) Rulers, according to the cynics, are simply thieves and tyrants masquerading as benefactors. Only fools would feel a *moral* obligation to obey the law under these circumstances. Only fools would voluntarily put the interests or judgment of the state above their own interests or judgment. Given their negative view of the state, it appears that cynics will obey the law when they must and disobey when they can get away with it.

The Anarchist Rejection of Government

Like the cynic, the anarchist rejects the idea that governments possess legitimate authority. Similarly, anarchists reject the idea that people should give special moral consideration to what the laws of the state require. While there are many different kinds of anarchism, all of them share a concern for preserving individual freedom and a distaste for the coercive measures of governments.

In thinking about anarchist attitudes toward government, it is important to see that the use of coercive powers is essential to the nature of government. Coercion involves forcing people to do what they do not want to do. Typically, governments do this by threatening to use force or impose punishments if a person does not follow its laws. Coercion, law, and government are, in fact, inextricably related. Indeed, laws have been defined as commands of the sovereign backed up by a threat.[8]

We can see the plausibility of this view by thinking of the difference between a tax and a charitable donation.

If I receive a request for money from a group engaged in famine relief or support of human rights, I can choose to make a donation or not. Even if I have a *moral* duty to support these activities, it is still up to me to decide whether I will do so. If I ignore the request, nothing will happen to me.

A tax, on the other hand, is entirely different. If I refuse to pay my taxes, then the government has the legal authority to use coercion to obtain my money. It can simply take the money without my consent by ordering my bank to deduct funds from my account. Or it can order my employer to deduct funds from my salary. Or it can seize my house, my car, or other property and sell them as a way of raising the equivalent funds. All these things can be done against my will. Alternatively, it may tell me that if I continue to refuse payment, then I will be fined or imprisoned. All of these methods involve coercion, imposing the government's decisions on me, even if it is against my will.

When we see that coercion is at the heart of government, then it becomes less mysterious why someone might embrace anarchism. Suppose that I want to use some portion of my money to buy a car or to contribute to famine relief efforts. Instead, however, the government requires that I pay it in taxes which are then used for a variety of activities. I may think that the uses to which the government puts my money are less good than the uses to which I would put it. Yet, given the coercive powers of the state, I will feel that I have no choice but to pay my taxes, even though this means that I cannot do the things I had wanted to do with my money.

Of course, there will be many occasions when a person's own judgment will agree with what the law requires, and on those occasions, anarchists will have no objection to doing what the law requires. So if I believe that it would be wrong for me to kill my best friend and if there are laws against murder, then anarchists will have no objection to my following the law. Notice, however, that in this case I am not refraining from murder *because* the law forbids it. For this reason, even though I am not disobeying the law, it is somewhat odd to say that I am obeying it. As Robert Paul Wolff, a defender of anarchism, points out, "Obedience is not a matter of doing what someone tells you to do. It is a matter of doing what he tells you to do *because he tells you to do it.*"[9] In not murdering my best friend, I am doing what *I* think is best, and this happens to coincide with what the law requires. So what the law says doesn't influence me at all. My behavior happens to conform to the law, but I am not really obeying or recognizing the law through my actions.

This point should make it clear that anarchists are not committed to trying to violate as many laws as possible. Rather, they want to be able to do what they think is best on all occasions, and they resent the fact that the government can coerce them into doing things they don't want to do or think are wrong. They reject the idea that governments have a right to exercise these coercive powers. For the anarchist, an ideal world would be one in which there were no governments to exercise these coercive powers. While this ideal has led some anarchists to attempt to destroy the state through violent action, this means of trying to bring about their ideal is not something that all anarchists would support. Indeed, some anarchists have been pacifists and thus have opposed all use of violence, whether by the state or by its opponents.

Like the political cynic, the anarchist would think that Socrates was making a terrible mistake in recognizing an obligation to obey the law and in sacrificing his life for his country. Of course, if Socrates wants to die and thinks that death is a desirable condition (as he suggests in the dialogue called the *Phaedo*), then there is no reason for him to escape. However, if he wants to live but remains in Athens and accepts death out of a sense that he has a moral duty to obey the law, then the anarchist would say he is making a costly error.

Anarchism, the belief in the ideal of no government, is an extreme and uncommon view. Most of us are "archists"—we believe in the legitimacy of governments. It may strike us as mysterious that anyone could actually be an anarchist. If we realize, however, that the existence of governments implies that some people have the right to force us to do what we don't want to do, then perhaps the real mystery is why so many of us think that governments really do have this authority. Like the cynic, anarchists will generally obey the law when they have to, but they won't like doing this, and they won't think of governments as valuable institutions that deserve our support.

There is one final point worth making about anarchists. Like the rest of us, anarchists can recognize that some governments are better than others. Some governments engage in widespread abuses of their citizens and make use of extensive and cruel forms of coercion. Other governments permit their citizens greater freedom and try to encourage compliance with the law through noncoercive means. Nonetheless, anarchists rightly insist that all governments, even the most benevolent of them, are coercive and claim the right to force citizens to do things against their will. It is because coercion is essential to the very nature of government that anarchists object to all governments, even though they may recognize that some governments are better or worse than others.

Martin Luther King and Critical Citizenship

The views we have looked at so far call for a single kind of outlook both toward government and toward the laws of the state. Socrates revered his state and defended an absolute obligation to obey its laws. Thrasymachus, Lenin, and other cynics see the state as a device for promoting the interests of those who hold power and thus urge contempt and hostility toward the state and its laws. Anarchists see coercive powers as the essence of government power and reject laws as illegitimate, seeing no obligation to obey them.

The attitude that I will call critical citizenship is opposed to all of these views. According to the critical citizenship position, laws and governments deserve our support and obedience only if they meet certain standards of justice and morality. For the critical citizen, whether a state deserves our loyalty depends on the kind of state it is, and whether we are morally obligated to obey the law depends on the kind of law that is in question. Allegiance to governments and the duty to obey laws is neither absolute nor unconditional. Both governments and laws must be worthy of our regard for them, and if they fail to be worthy, we are under no obligation to obey them.

This view is powerfully expressed by Martin Luther King, Jr., in his "Letter from Birmingham City Jail." King wrote his letter to a group of white clergymen who had criticized his use of illegal action as a means of protesting laws that restricted the rights of black people. He wrote the letter in April 1963, after having been arrested himself and while he was confined in the jail in Birmingham, Alabama.

The crucial feature of the position King puts forward in this letter is the element of *selective* obedience and disobedience. Whether one is morally obligated to obey a law depends on the nature of the law itself. If the law is imposed by a tyrannical government and requires actions that are immoral, then we have no obligation to obey. However, if a good government passes laws that serve people's legitimate interests and violate no one's rights, then obedience to the law is morally obligatory.

At one level, this view seems obviously right. At another level, however, this view is quite problematic, for it is hard to see how to distinguish it from the view of the cynic or anarchist, both of whom will sometimes do what the law says but neither of whom is willing to recognize any obligation to obey the law. One might ask how one can talk about people having an obligation to obey the law if the people themselves get to pick and choose which laws to obey and which laws to violate.

Since King had both spoken of the need to obey some laws and called for violating other laws, he was criticized for being inconsistent about the duty to obey the law. Addressing his critics, he wrote:

> You express a great deal of anxiety over our willingness to break laws. This is certainly a legitimate concern. Since we so diligently urge people to obey the Supreme Court's decision of 1954 outlawing segregation in the public schools, it is rather strange and paradoxical to find us consciously breaking laws. One may well ask, "How can you advocate breaking some laws and obeying others?"[10]

King replies to this charge by distinguishing two types of laws and differentiating the obligations that attach to each.

> There are *just* laws and there are *unjust* laws. I would be the first to advocate obeying just laws. One has not only a legal but moral responsibility to obey just laws. Conversely, one has a moral responsibility to disobey unjust laws.[11]

If there are different types of laws, then one could advocate that some laws be obeyed and other laws disobeyed without contradicting oneself. This is what King does.

For the advocate of critical citizenship, then, there is no blanket yes or no answer to our questions about whether governments should be supported and laws obeyed. The critical citizen replies that "it all depends." It depends on the nature of the government and the nature of the laws. King thought that he could in good conscience disobey laws upholding racial segregation. These laws were immoral because the practice of segregation "ends up relegating persons to the status of things." The law that called for school integration, however, was a morally good law that "uplifts human personality."[12]

The difficulty with King's position is that it leaves it up to individuals to determine which laws are just and which are unjust. Yet this discretionary power may seem to be inconsistent with the obligatory and coercive nature of law. The difference between a law and a recommendation is a difference between a matter of choice and a matter of necessity. We pass laws precisely because we don't want individuals exercising discretion on some matters, and if everyone does exercise such discretion, then one may think there is in fact no law operating at all. As we have seen, this is precisely the challenge that the Laws put to Socrates in the *Crito,* saying, "Do you imagine that a state can subsist and not be overthrown, in which the decisions of law have no power, but are set aside and overthrown by individuals?"[13] Matters are made worse when, as was the case with racial segregation, there are serious differences of opinion between people. In such cases, allowing everyone to decide for themselves whether to obey or disobey the law would seem to threaten us with chaos.

So the selective position recommended by King raises some difficult questions, even though it may appear to be a simple, commonsense view.

Making Our Own Choice

Each of the views I have described has some plausibility. There are probably times when each of us, like Socrates, thinks that our country and its laws deserve our unswerving support, even when we disagree with particular judgments or decisions. We think it wrong if others don't see this and claim for themselves the right to decide whether they should be subject to rules that apply to everyone. On other occasions, however, we may look distrustfully at those in power and wonder whether they care about our well-being at all. On such occasions, like the cynic, we will think that we owe them neither respect nor obedience. Or, like the anarchist, we may simply think that we should do whatever we ourselves think is best and that there is no reason to attach any special importance to laws and governments. Finally, there are times when it seems obviously correct, as the critical citizenship view says, that under some circumstances people do owe allegiance and obedience, while under other circumstances these are inappropriate.

In working out our own views and choosing an appropriate political outlook, we want to see whether we can arrive at one consistent view, rather than simply having different and conflicting attitudes at different times. After all, it is obviously impossible for all of these views to be correct. So it would be good to know which of them is right.

It is possible, of course, that there is some view other than the four I have considered that is the correct one. I do not want to claim that these are the only possibilities. However, these views seem to capture the main options that are available. For example, if we ask whether governments ever have legitimate authority, there would appear to be a small set of possible answers. One can answer "Yes, they always do," which is the answer of super patriotism, or "No, they never do," which is the answer of anarchists and some cynics. Or one can say "Sometimes they do, and sometimes they don't," which is the answer of some cynics and of critical citizenship advocates.[14] No other answers are possible.

Likewise, if we ask whether citizens have a moral duty to obey the law, there is a similar set of possibilities. "Yes, they have a duty always to obey," say the super patriots. "No, they never have a duty to obey," say the anarchists and some cynics. And "Sometimes they have a duty to obey and sometimes not," say the critical citizenship advocates.

So only a small set of basic answers to these questions is possible, and the four views I have described seem to express these basic possibilities. Different thinkers will, of course, develop and defend these basic views in their own individual ways. Nonetheless, even if refinements and variations on these outlooks are possible, our discussion will be covering the basic options. We can be confident that no basic types of options are being omitted because the four views cover the logically possible set of basic answers to the questions we are considering.

Which of them, then, is the strongest and most reasonable view? Which outlook should you or I adopt? In the next chapters I will examine each of these four views in order to try to answer these questions.

Notes

1. Plato, "Crito," trans. Benjamin Jowett, in *The Dialogues of Plato* (New York: Random House, 1937), vol. 1, 434.
2. Ibid., 434–435.
3. Plato, *The Republic of Plato,* trans. F. M. Cornford (New York: Oxford University Press, 1945), 18.
4. Ibid.
5. Ibid., 25.
6. V. I. Lenin, "State and Revolution," in *Social and Political Philosophy,* eds. J. Somerville and R. Santoni (Garden City, NY: Doubleday [Anchor Books], 1963), 383.
7. Ibid., 411.
8. This definition, associated with the British thinker John Austin, is discussed and criticized in J. Murphy and J. Coleman, *The Philosophy of Law* (Totowa, NJ: Rowman and Allanheld, 1984), 22–38; and in Martin Golding, *Philosophy of Law* (Englewood Cliffs, NJ: Prentice-Hall, 1975), 24–29.
9. R. P. Wolff, *In Defense of Anarchism* (New York: Harper & Row, 1970), 9.
10. M. L. King, Jr., "Letter from Birmingham City Jail," in *Nonviolence in America: A Documentary History,* ed. S. Lynd (Indianapolis: Bobbs-Merrill, 1966), 467–468.
11. Ibid., 468.
12. Ibid.
13. Plato, "The Crito," 434.
14. The different forms of political cynicism will be explained in Chapter 3.

Super Patriotism

IN THIS CHAPTER I WANT TO RETURN TO THE SUPER PATRIOTISM expressed by Socrates in the *Crito* in order to examine the idea that all of us have an absolute obligation to obey the law. It is important to see that this view is not just limited to Socrates or his contemporaries in ancient Athens. The same view is expressed in the familiar saying, "My country, right or wrong." Moreover, it appears to be the view of those people who condemned Martin Luther King for urging that people disobey unjust laws and use civil disobedience as a way to protest racial segregation. Anyone who thinks that even unjust laws should be obeyed must believe that there is a powerful obligation to obey the law.

What arguments could one use to justify this view?

In the *Crito* Socrates gives three main arguments for this view. These arguments are put forward in a long speech that Socrates imagines the Laws directing at him. He summarizes the main points as follows:

> [H]e who disobeys us [the laws] is, as we maintain, thrice wrong; first, because in disobeying us he is disobeying his parents; secondly, because we are the authors of his education [i.e., his benefactors]; thirdly, because he has made an agreement with us that he will duly obey our commands; and he neither obeys them nor convinces us that our commands are wrong. . . .[1]

Each of the three arguments summarized is supposed to support the conclusion that it would be morally wrong for Socrates to disobey the law.

In analyzing these arguments, we can see that each one begins with a relevant fact about Socrates. The first argument highlights the fact that the state is Socrates' *parent,* the second that the state is Socrates' educator or *benefactor,* and the third that Socrates has made an *agreement* to obey the law. In addition, each argument implicitly assumes some general principle about what people are morally obligated to do. The first assumes that everyone ought to obey his parents, the second that everyone ought to obey his benefactors, and the third that everyone ought to keep his agreements.

If we set out the argument in a way that makes each part of them fully explicit, we get the following results:

The Parent Argument

1. The state is Socrates' parent.
2. Everyone ought to obey his parents.
3. The state has commanded that Socrates be punished.
4. If Socrates escapes, he will disobey his parent.
5. Therefore, Socrates ought not to escape.

The Benefactor Argument

1. The state is Socrates' benefactor.
2. Everyone ought to obey his benefactors.
3. The state has commanded that Socrates be punished.
4. If Socrates escapes, he will disobey his benefactor.
5. Therefore, Socrates ought not to escape.

The Agreement Argument

1. Socrates made an agreement to obey the state.
2. Everyone ought to keep his agreements.
3. The state has commanded that Socrates be punished.
4. If Socrates escapes, he will violate an agreement.
5. Therefore, Socrates ought not to escape.

Each of these arguments has the same form, but they differ because each one focuses on a different relationship that exists between Socrates and the state, and each one appeals to a different moral principle. Each of them is supposed to demonstrate that it would be wrong for Socrates to escape from prison because that would violate his obligation to obey the law.

Do these arguments prove that Socrates is morally obligated not to escape from prison?

The Parent Argument

The idea that the state is Socrates' parent may at first strike us as absurd. The state is not a living organism, so it cannot either conceive or bear children. For this reason, it makes no sense to think of the relationship between citizens and the state as a biological one.

In spite of this apparent foolishness, the idea that Socrates asserts here is a powerful one. Most of us, after all, are citizens of states that we are born into. We did not choose the society to which we belong. Indeed, the fact that we are born in one place rather than another determines many of the fundamental facts about our-selves and our lives. It determines what language we speak and even, to some extent, what facial or bodily gestures we use to express our feelings. It determines many of our attitudes about food, health, about what goals are worth pursuing, and about what actions are legitimate to perform. So while the state may not be our biological parent, it is not merely metaphoric to say that our nature as people is at least partly created by the soci-ety into which we are born.

These facts are reflected in our language. The word *patriotism* derives from *pater,* the Latin word for father. In addition, we are all familiar with expressions like *father-land, motherland,* and *mother tongue,* even if they are no longer part of our common speech.

Let us grant, then, that Socrates is saying something significant when he asserts that the state is his parent, even if this is false in the literal, biological sense of the word *parent.* Even if we grant Socrates this point, how-ever, his argument fails to prove that we ought always to obey the state's commands. There are two important rea-sons why the argument fails.

First, if Socrates' idea is that people ought to obey whatever parents they are born to, this does not seem plausible. Suppose that my biological parents abandoned me at birth and never took care of me. It is implausible to suggest that I would have any obligation to them what-soever. My birth seems to have been a mere accident, and the fact that certain people are my parents does not indicate that they have any concern for my well-being. Suppose further that someone other than my biological parents has raised and cared for me. In such a case, what-ever obligations exist would be owed to the adoptive par-ent and not the biological ones.

Or suppose that parents do raise a child but treat the child very badly, abusing it and making use of it only as a source of income or other benefits for them-selves. Here again, the parent/child relationship would not give rise to any obligations or duties on the part of the child.

The parent argument presupposes what we normally take for granted, that people who have children will love them and provide for them. This does not always happen, however, and when it does not, then the child has no obligation toward the biological parents. Whatever obligation we owe to parents is *conditional* on how they treat us. Our duties to our parents depend on how they carried out their duties as parents. So Socrates is wrong to assert unconditionally that the state's being our parent makes us obligated to obey it.

There is a second problem. Even if we assume both that parents have done their best in raising and caring for a child and that the child does have obligations to the parents, it does not follow that the child has an *unlimited* obligation to obey. Suppose that a parent commands a child to kill or injure an innocent person. The mere fact that the parent commands this action does not make it right and does not make it an obligation. There are limits to what parents may legitimately command. These limits derive both from the rights of the child (beyond a certain age) to determine his or her own actions and from the rights of other people, which may be violated by the action commanded. Whether we have an obligation to obey a command depends not only on *who* issues the command but also on *what* the command tells us to do.

For both of these reasons, then, it appears to be false that there is an absolute obligation to do what one's parents command.

Both of the objections I have raised against the parent argument are, in a sense, abstract ones. That is, they are general objections to the idea that children have an unconditional, unlimited obligation to obey their parents. In addition, however, these problems are directly relevant to Socrates' situation, since it is plausible to argue that his false conviction and his harsh sentence represent a form of bad treatment by the state. Likewise, it is plausible to claim that even if he has some obligation to obey the state, his own right to protect his life shows that he is not obligated to accept death as a punishment for a crime he did not commit.

Socrates' first argument, then, is not a strong one, even if we accept his premise that his relationship to the state is similar to the relation he has with his parents.

The Benefactor Argument

Socrates' second argument appeals to the fact that the state has done many good things for him, providing him with an education and other goods necessary for his development and his living a satisfactory life. Having benefited from his relation to the state, Socrates claims that he has an obligation to obey it.

This is plausible. We often feel indebted to people who have been kind or generous to us or to anyone who has made it possible for us to enjoy significant goods. Many people believe that political obligations arise from this relationship. Since we have benefited from the state, it is important for us to reciprocate with our obedience, respect, and support.

While this argument has a great deal of plausibility, it is not without its problems. First, it is not clear that receiving benefits always generates obligations. Suppose that a wealthy person decides to make a yearly deposit in my bank account, beginning when I reach the age of five. After doing this for many years, the person comes to me and commands that I work for his company. Surely I am not obligated to do so. I might feel grateful for the goods I've received, but I did not ask for them and did not know that they came with strings attached. Moreover, since the benefits began when I was quite young, I was in no position at the time to ask if something would be expected of me in return, and I was in no position to make a rational judgment about whether to accept these benefits.

Again, this is rather like the position of an individual citizen. If we live in a good society, we begin to receive benefits from the society from a very early age. Even if others agree that there are obligations that arise from benefiting in this way, we ourselves are not free to determine whether we approve of this sort of arrangement. So it seems unfair to say, "You took these benefits, and now you owe us your obedience." All of us, for at least part of our lives, receive benefits through no choice of our own and with no understanding of whether obligations arise from our acceptance.

Furthermore, even if our benefiting from the state does generate some obligation, it is hard to accept that it is an unlimited obligation. It is hard to believe that we are obligated to obey the state that has benefited us, no matter what it commands us. If a benefactor commands me to kill an innocent person or to submit to torture, complying would violate my rights or the rights of the intended victim. In these cases, I ought *not* to obey because what is being commanded is immoral. So even if there is a general obligation to obey benefactors (which I have suggested need not be true), it is false that this is an unlimited obligation.

Finally, the facts of Socrates' case are again relevant. At the time of his decision, he is awaiting what he believes to be an unjust punishment. The state, which had been his benefactor, is now threatening his life. It is a benefactor no longer, and one might plausibly believe that the state's present behavior frees Socrates from whatever obligation he previously might have had to it.

The Agreement Argument

The agreement argument is likely to strike us as the strongest of Socrates' arguments. There are good reasons for this, for it is immune to some of the weaknesses of the parent argument and the benefactor argument.

While we cannot choose our parents or decide during childhood whether to accept benefits, we do have control over the agreements we enter into. Agreements are voluntary in a way that receiving benefits from someone may not be and that being born to someone never is. Moreover, in making an agreement, we usually understand what the conditions of the agreement are. (If we don't understand them, then we are not really agreeing to them.) We know what we are getting into, what we can expect of others, and what they can expect of us. If we know all these things and enter into the agreement, then it seems fair to say that we are morally obligated to carry it out. So if Socrates has agreed to obey the laws, then he may well have a genuine obligation to do so.

Before considering this argument directly, we need to look at the kind of agreement that Socrates made. Agreements can be classified as either explicit or tacit. An explicit agreement is made when a person signs on the dotted line, says "I do," or in some other way explicitly accepts the terms of an agreement. A tacit agreement is one that a person makes implicitly by virtue of taking part in activities or not openly objecting to something. Someone who enters a golf tournament, for example, tacitly agrees to count every shot and to refrain from actions like moving the ball to give herself an easier shot to the green. Similarly, a person who does not object when the chair of a meeting says "Is this okay with everyone?" has tacitly accepted whatever was being proposed.

Although Socrates says that he "above all other men . . . acknowledged the agreement [with the state],"[2] his agreement is in fact a tacit one. For the main indicator of agreement was his remaining in Athens throughout his life rather than choosing to go elsewhere. Thus the laws tell him:

[W]e . . . proclaim and give the right to every Athenian, that if he does not like us when he has come of age and has seen the ways of the city, and made our acquaintance, he may go where he pleases and take

> his goods with him. . . . But he who has experience of
> the manner in which we order justice and administer
> the state, and still remains has entered into an implied
> contract that he will do as we command him.[3]

Socrates not only remained in Athens when entering
manhood, he spent his whole life there, never leaving
except for military service. He never went off to attend
festivals or to see what other cities were like. Moreover,
even at his trial, when he could have proposed exile instead of death as a punishment, he did not do so. So, the
laws tell him, "[You] had seventy years to think . . . during which time you were at liberty to leave the city . . . if
our covenants appeared to you to be unfair."[4]

Criticizing the
Agreement Argument

Several questions need to be raised about the agreement
argument: First, does remaining in a place constitute a
tacit agreement to obey its laws? Second, if remaining in
a place does constitute an agreement to obey the laws,
does it obligate one to do whatever the state commands?
Finally, if remaining in a place does constitute an agreement to obey the laws, does it obligate one to obey under all conditions?

For Socrates' argument to work, all of these questions must be answered affirmatively. If we decide that
any of them should be answered negatively, then
Socrates' argument will be undermined. I believe that
the right answer to all of these questions is no, and I will
now try to show why this is the case.

First, Socrates argues that simply by staying in Athens
when he could have left, he thereby made an agreement
to obey its laws. In considering this, it is important to
remember that this is not because of any special facts
about Socrates. Rather, as the speech by the laws makes
clear, it depends on the general principle that anyone

who may leave a place but chooses to remain there tacitly agrees to obey its laws. Is this true?

Imagine a person who lives in a country with repressive laws and a corrupt regime. As she comes of age, she realizes the nature of the regime, but she decides not to leave the country. Why? Because her family and friends live there, because the language, customs, and traditions are familiar, because it is a place of great natural beauty. To go elsewhere would require leaving family and friends, learning a new and unfamiliar language, adapting to new customs, and cutting herself off from favorite places and natural beauties.

So she stays, but she does so in spite of the laws and the government and perhaps with a feeling of bitterness that she and her fellow citizens must live under such a regime. While this person remains in her country and does not take advantage of the right to leave it, the reason she does so is that the costs of leaving are extremely high. Her remaining does not indicate her approval or willing acceptance of the laws or government. She would be willing to agree to a just system, but she neither supports nor agrees to the one in power.

In this sort of case, remaining in a country does not express approval for the laws, and it is implausible to state that it constitutes a tacit agreement to obey them. Similarly, if a person does not object to a proposal at a meeting because he fears that he will be attacked for doing so, then his silence is coerced and does not constitute tacit approval.

No doubt Socrates' situation was not exactly like the one I have described. His personal relationship to Athens was by and large positive. He had great affection for the city, though in fact he did not always approve of those who governed it. In any case, whether Socrates' relationship to his city was positive or negative, what my example shows is that he is wrong to assume that by choosing to remain in a place, a person tacitly agrees to obey its laws and government.

A second problem concerns Socrates' assumption that agreeing to obey the laws is the same as agreeing to do whatever the state tells him to do. These need not be the same. A person might be willing to do her fair share as a citizen and to accept the burdens of limiting her actions to those that are legal. Part of her expectation in making this agreement is that as long as she obeys the laws, she will not be deprived of her rights by the state. Suppose, however, that she obeys the laws conscientiously, but, either through error or the malice of officials, she is convicted of a crime and sentenced to a harsh punishment. It is hard to believe that her prior agreement to obey the laws obligates her to accept an unwarranted punishment. It is one thing to agree to play by the rules in the expectation that one will enjoy the immunities of innocence and quite another thing to think that one has a duty to accept undeserved punishments when these are commanded by the state. To require this is to go beyond what can reasonably be expected of a person. Even if the first obligation—to obey the laws—grows out of remaining in a country, the second—to do whatever the state says—does not.

Finally, Socrates argues that the agreement a citizen makes obligates him to obey under all conditions. Suppose, however, that we view the state's unjust conviction and punishment as violations of the agreement it made with him. If we do, then it is plausible to argue that, under these conditions, citizens are freed of their obligation to uphold their part of the contract. In general, when one party to an agreement breaks the agreement, the other party is relieved of the obligation it had. If, for example, a company agrees to deliver equipment to another company on a certain date for a specified sum of money and if the money is not paid, then the company is relieved of its duty to deliver the equipment. Likewise, if Socrates' conviction constitutes a violation of the agreement he made with the state, then he may no longer be bound to obey it.

In spite of its plausibility, then, Socrates' appeal to a tacit agreement with the state does not prove that he is bound to remain in prison and accept the punishment that awaits him. A plausible case can be made for thinking, first, that remaining in a place does not constitute a tacit agreement; second, that even if it did, the agreement to obey the laws does not mean that one is also bound to accept unjust punishments; and third, that unjust treatment of a citizen by the state can be seen as a violation of the agreement that relieves the citizen of his obligation to continue holding to the agreement.

There is one final and important point about the tacit agreement argument. A serious problem with tacit agreements is that they are vague. In an explicit agreement, there is at least the possibility of stating exactly what is being agreed to. A well-written contract will make clear just what each of the parties is bound to do and under what conditions the contract is no longer binding. A tacit agreement of the sort Socrates made is entirely unclear. Unless there were strong prior understandings that were widely understood, then even if we regard remaining in a country as a tacit agreement, it will be unclear just what is being agreed to. Indeed, different citizens might have different understandings of their duty to the state and if their obligations are in part determined by how they interpret the implied contract, then different citizens might actually be agreeing to different things and have different obligations. So even if we accept the general form of Socrates' agreement argument, we need not accept the specific content that he believed was part of the contract between the state and its citizens.

The Super Patriotic Attitude

What is central to super patriotism is the belief in an unconditional and unlimited obligation to do what the state says. I have tried to show that the arguments Socrates provides for this view do not justify it and that it is implausible to believe in such a powerful obligation to the state.

One might think that even if I have refuted Socrates' arguments for this view, this does not matter because his views were voiced so long ago and so much has changed since his death in 399 B.C. What is remarkable about Socrates' arguments, however, is that they are basically the same ones we hear from people today when they try to justify their belief that citizens have very powerful obligations to their governments.

We have all heard people justifying their loyalty by saying, "I was born here, and this is my country." This is essentially Socrates' parent argument, that just as being born to certain parents makes for special duties to them, so being born in a particular country makes for special duties to it.

Likewise, we have all heard people say, "I owe so much to my country; it has done so much for me. I am indebted to it for my education or the freedom to pursue my own goals." This is essentially the benefactor argument that Socrates put forward.

Finally, when people reply to protesters and critics of government policy with the slogan "Love it or leave it," they are claiming that a person who remains in a country must accept its policies and that someone who does not like the policies should leave the country. What the slogan implies is that remaining in a country tacitly commits one to supporting its policies or, as the laws told Socrates, to doing whatever it commands. Those who refuse to agree to this must leave.

Since these contemporary views are variations on the arguments Socrates gave and since we have seen that Socrates' arguments fail to justify unconditional and unlimited obedience to government, we can conclude that these contemporary expressions of super patriotism also fail to justify it as an appropriate attitude for us to take toward government.

This is not to say that we have no obligation to obey the law and no obligation to support our government.

Such obligations may well exist, but they do not exist in the very powerful form that Socrates and other super patriots defend.

Some people believe that in rejecting super patriotism, we automatically commit ourselves to denying that any political obligations exist. Even if they are right, however, this does not support super patriotism. It may only show that indeed there are no political obligations, that no one has any obligations to governments or to the law. The next three chapters will examine political cynicism and anarchism, two views that explicitly call into question whether there are any political obligations.

Notes

1. Plato, "The Crito," 435–436.
2. Ibid., 436.
3. Ibid., 435.
4. Ibid., 436.

CHAPTER 3

Political Cynicism

POLITICAL CYNICS VIEW GOVERNMENT WITH A KNOWING AND scornful attitude. While others are taken in by talk of patriotism, national unity, political obligations, and ideals of citizenship, cynics claim to see through to what they say is the true situation—that government is an institution for benefiting those who govern and for using those who are governed to promote the interests of the governing elite.

Some people may be inspired by words like those of President John Kennedy when he said, "Ask not what your country can do for you. Ask what you can do for your country." For cynics, this statement expresses an important truth but not the noble one that others hear. Cynics think that all appeals to work for the well-being of the country are merely covers for getting citizens to work against their own interests. Hence, Kennedy's statement was, in an ironic way, accurate. He was telling people that they should not expect benefits from the country. Rather, they should be working to benefit the country, and in doing so, cynics say, they will actually be benefiting those who govern.

Cynics have a radically different view of the function of government from most of us. Most of us think that government exists to serve the people. Even if we acknowledge that officials sometimes take advantage of their positions to benefit themselves, we see this as an aberration, a departure from the true purpose of government. What Thrasymachus, Lenin, and other cynics claim, however, is that the true function of government is to benefit those in power. Hence, when we discover officials using their power for their own good or to benefit their friends, this is no accident or departure from the norm. This is government acting for its true purpose.

The cynic's view of the state is nicely expressed in a short parable told by Robert Paul Wolff. He writes:

> A band of robbers ride into town with guns drawn and demand all the gold in the bank. They are called criminals. They return the next year on the same day and repeat their demand. Again they are called criminals. They put on uniforms and return each year on the same day. Eventually, they are called tax collectors. Finally, the smallest and least offensive of the bandits rides into town unarmed and the townspeople give him their gold without a struggle. The state has arrived.[1]

This little story nicely captures the central core of the cynic's view of the state.

If this is the truth about the state, however, why is the contrary belief so widespread? Why do so many people think that governments have legitimate authority and that they act for the public interest? The answer is simple. People in government devote a great deal of effort to spreading this view—through speeches, public ceremonies, education, and other forms of communication—because it makes the public more compliant. It is difficult to rule people by force alone. It is much easier to rule them if they can be brought to believe that the government possesses some form of legitimacy. This is done by telling people such things as that government is "of the people, by the people, and for the people," or that the purpose of government is to "establish justice, insure domestic tranquility, provide for the common defense, promote the general welfare, and secure the blessings of liberty. . . . " If people believe these sorts of things, they will be more likely to obey laws, pay taxes, and even give their lives in war when the government tells them to. Believing this, they may even actively want to make these sacrifices, just as Socrates actively wanted to give his life for his country by suffering a punishment that he could have avoided.

The Moral Force of Cynicism

The cynic's vision is a powerful one, and it is clearly relevant to the question of how we should view our duties as citizens. If things are as cynics describe them, then the devotion to the state exemplified by Socrates and others who have made significant sacrifices for their governments is totally misguided.

We can see why it is misguided by looking once again at two of Socrates' arguments. Socrates claimed that he owed obedience to the state because it was his benefactor. Suppose that this is true and that the state has actually benefited him. Suppose further, however, that the state is not really interested in his well-being and benefits him but only enough to keep him thinking that it cares about his individual well-being. Suppose that it could benefit him more but chooses not to in order to increase "profits" to those in power. Or suppose that it benefits him but only so that he can contribute to it. It educates and trains him, but only so that he can be productive, pay taxes, and defend the country in time of war. The benefits he receives are not provided for his sake. Instead, they are provided because benefiting him advances the interests of the rulers themselves.

If this is the motive that leads the state to act as a benefactor, then it seems odd to claim that a citizen should feel indebted to the government. To return to an analogy used by Thrasymachus, a citizen who felt indebted to the state in this situation would be like a sheep who felt indebted to the shepherd for his food. Given that the food is provided simply to fatten the sheep for slaughter, a feeling of obligation or devotion would be quite inappropriate.

The cynical view of the aims and motives of those in power undermines the "benefit argument" by showing that whatever benefits are enjoyed by a person do not arise out of any concern for the citizen himself. The benefits are given only to increase his compliance with the law or to make him a more valuable instrument for pursuing the interests of those in power. From the perspective of the state (according to cynics), individual citizens are not ends in themselves but are rather human resources in which the rulers may invest, but always with their own goals and purposes in mind. In this context, benefits do not generate obligations.

Likewise, Socrates' appeal to the idea of a tacit agreement loses much of its force from the perspective of the cynic's view of government. Even if citizens do tacitly agree to obey the law, they do this only because they misunderstand either the nature of the agreement or the system to which they are agreeing. No rational person would choose to make an agreement that gave some people extraordinary power over others in order that those people might enrich and empower themselves at the expense of others. It is one thing to give some people special powers so that they can protect the community and its citizens. This might well be rational to agree to, but it is entirely different to imagine agreeing to an arrangement that gives some people special powers so that they can use the community for their own benefit. That would be like voluntarily agreeing to become a slave.

If we couple the logic of the "agreement argument" with the facts as the cynic portrays them, then it is clear that no one would willingly become a party to such an agreement. No one would recognize the state as legitimate. The cynic's image of things is clearly relevant to our assessing the legitimacy of the state and the nature of whatever obligations we might (or might not) have toward it.

Types of Cynicism

The cynic's view of government seems simple, but there are actually a number of different versions of political cynicism. It is important to differentiate these versions because they suggest different kinds of responses that one might adopt.

The first distinction is between what I shall call the *local cynic* and the *universal cynic*. The local cynic looks at his own government and believes that it is organized to benefit the rulers. The universal cynic believes that all governments are organized in this way.

How one responds to the cynical view depends in part on which interpretation one takes. If one is a local cynic and believes that his own rulers are out for themselves, then one may decide to emigrate to a better place where rulers actually try to serve their community. If one is a universal cynic, however, then this strategy will make no sense because all governments will be alike in their aims and functions. They will all exist simply to benefit those in power. So, according to universal cynicism, there is no place to escape to, no place in which government serves citizens.

The second distinction is between what I shall call *necessary cynicism* and *contingent cynicism*. According to the "necessary" view, all governments are by nature exploitative. Governments are necessarily exploitative in the same way that triangles are necessarily three-sided. According to the "contingent" version of cynicism, some or all governments might be exploitative, but it is at least possible for governments to be benevolent in their aims and functions. Necessary cynicism does not allow that it is even possible for a government to be benevolent rather than exploitative.

Putting together the two sets of distinctions, we can see that the necessary view implies the universal view. That is, if it is necessarily true that government is exploitative, then all governments will be exploitative. If the contingent view is true, however, then it may turn out that some governments are exploitative while others are not. Thus, the local form of cynicism and the contingent form are more natural partners, for both imply the possibility of benevolent and just governments, even if it turns out (contingently) that there are none. The local and contingent forms of the theory hold out the promise that there may be better places to move to or that governments may be improved to make them more subservient to the needs of citizens. According to the necessary view, all attempts to find or to form a government that is dedicated to the common good are doomed to failure. A nonexploitative government is no more possible than a non-three-sided triangle.

Having sorted out these distinctions, we are now in a better position to understand the practical implications of the cynical view. If one decides that government is exploitative and that Thrasymachus was right to call justice "the interest of the stronger," then what political attitudes or actions might one adopt?

The Lives of Cynics

One response to the cynical view is to attempt to do the best one can for oneself within a basically exploitative system. If one is only concerned about oneself, then the best position would be to become one of the rulers and to use the state for one's own good. The ideal situation, from this point of view, is to become one of the exploiters rather than one of the exploited. In Plato's *The Republic*, Thrasymachus makes clear that this is an enviable position. If justice is the interest of the stronger, then, according to this view, one should seek to be among the strong and to take advantage of the system to advance one's own interests.

If it is impossible to become a ruler, then a rational cynic will certainly feel no obligation to obey the laws, but she will do so when it is in her interests. Fear of punishment will often lead to law-abiding actions, and the prospect of reward might even motivate what look like patriotic actions. Essentially, one would make the best of the situation, trying to improve one's private life as much as possible.

If one cannot lead an acceptable life within the system, then one might think about emigration to another place. As we have seen, however, this strategy only makes sense if one is a local cynic. If one thinks that all governments are exploitative, then emigration will not solve the problem.

Likewise, if life within the system is unacceptable, one might try to change the system. This approach may seem inconsistent with cynicism, but it is not. Even if the universal and necessary forms of cynicism are correct that all governments are necessarily exploitative, it does not follow that the system cannot be changed. After all, there are degrees of exploitation. Not every exploitative government is equally bad. Some governments may be able to get away with greater exploitation of their citizens than others.

Even on the most pessimistic cynical views, then, while governments cannot be transformed into instruments to serve the people, people may nonetheless bring about improvement through various forms of pressure or protest. Rulers may not be benevolent, but they may be forced to provide benefits or diminish the exploitation of people in order to win their cooperation.

One possible response to cynicism, then, is to seek reform. The most optimistic reformer will believe that government can be transformed into a device for promoting the general welfare. A more pessimistic reformer will believe that while the system will always be exploitative, it can at least be changed so as to make it less abusive and harsh or to make it provide more benefits to people.

A local cynic can actually be a political idealist. He can be cynical about the actions of the current government but quite idealistic about the possibilities for reform. He may think that if only different people were given power, then things would be better. Or that if a better constitution could be adopted, things would improve. We tend to reserve the term *cynic* for those who see government as exploitative and who believe that no improvement is possible, but a person could agree with the cynic about the evils of a current government and yet be optimistic about the possibility for change and improvement. So cynicism about the actual situation can give rise to the impulse to reform and improve.

Cynicism and Anarchy

Suppose, however, that one believes that no serious reform of government is possible, that even if, for example, democratic procedures are introduced, this will make no difference. This would be to hold the universal, necessary versions of cynicism in their most extreme pessimistic forms. Governments, in this view, cannot be changed from the exploitative role that they play. Nor can their bad effects on people's lives be significantly diminished.

One might think that this bleak perspective would lead to political passivity and a desire simply to look out for oneself. To think this is to overlook one possibility, however: the possibility that government itself might be destroyed and that people would live without any government at all. According to this view, government cannot be improved, but improvement can be won by destroying government and living without it.

This is the approach taken by various anarchist thinkers. They accept the cynics' view that governments are necessarily exploitative and the pessimists' view that they cannot be improved. Finding life under government to be intolerable, however, they argue that we should attempt to reconstruct life without government institutions.

This view is part of Marxist thinking and is clearly expressed by Lenin in *State and Revolution*. Lenin argued that the state is (necessarily) an instrument by which one class, the bourgeoisie or property owners, oppresses another, the proletariat or workers. Suppose, however, that the class structure of society is destroyed by a Communist revolution. Then a classless society would exist, and there would no longer be a function for the state. Citing Marx and Engel's comments, Lenin claims that in a classless society, the state will "wither away." Deprived of its function (the oppression of one class by another), the state would have nothing to do and would cease to exist.[2]

Lenin's view combines a variety of the ideas that we have considered. He accepts the cynic's view that government is universally and necessarily exploitative. He rejects the possibility of reforming government, but he nonetheless thinks that improvement is possible through the destruction of government and the class system it enforces. His final goal is a utopian condition of anarchy.

What is interesting about Lenin's view is the way it combines elements of thought that seem incompatible with one another: extreme cynicism about present governments, deep pessimism about peaceful reform, and extraordinary optimism about the post-revolutionary, anarchic condition. Without classes and without government, he assures us, all would be well.[3]

Lenin believed that class society and government could be destroyed and anarchy achieved only through violent revolution. It is important to see, however, that one could accept his cynicism, his pessimism about reform, and his anarchist vision of the future and still reject his views about the necessity for violent revolution. Instead, one might think that the downfall of a government could be brought about by widespread refusals to cooperate with the government. Advocates of nonviolent change, like Gandhi, stress the degree to which governments require the assent of people and cannot control everyone by violent means. They argue that if large numbers of people simply refuse to pay taxes, for example, or to serve in the army or to cooperate with officials in any way, then no government could survive. This would be a nonviolent revolutionary strategy.[4]

Still another possibility for cynics is the gradual erosion of governmental legitimacy and power as people come to believe that governments are evil and slowly evolve ways of handling problems that do not require government institutions. Over time, the government would "wither away," according to this view, but there would be no violent attack on the government, no attempt to destroy it by force as Lenin and other advocates of revolutionary violence have sought to do. Lenin's commitment to violence is not required either by his cynicism, his pessimism about reform, or his utopian anarchism.

Is Cynicism True?

As we have seen, there are in fact several different forms of political cynicism, so there is no simple answer to the question of whether "it" is true. Nonetheless, there is a core set of beliefs common to all cynics. These are:

1. The central function of at least some governments is to benefit those who rule by exploiting those who are ruled.
2. Governments that exploit citizens in this way do not have political legitimacy.
3. Citizens have no obligation to respect or obey these governments.

Beyond this core, cynics differ considerably, both in the extent of the claim they want to make about how governments actually operate and in their recommendations for how we ought to behave in light of the facts they reveal.

If we want to evaluate the cynic's view, we need to know whether the central function of government actually is to benefit those in power. We cannot tell whether this cynical description of the facts is true, however, just by thought and reflection. In order to know whether a government serves the interests of those in power or is dedicated to the common good, we need to examine the facts and see how that government actually behaves. In some cases, governments may be crudely exploitative, and this may be evident to all because ordinary people are routinely killed or tortured, because the country's assets are transferred to private bank accounts controlled by the rulers, and because force is the primary means by which the government retains power. This is, unfortunately, not an uncommon situation, as the reports of human rights groups like Amnesty International make clear. Local cynics are without doubt correct about at least some governments.

In the case of other governments, the evidence may be less clear. Civil rights and participation in government may be extended to citizens, and some policies may clearly benefit ordinary people. Yet, at the same time, others in power may gain a larger share of the benefits, and one might suppose that democratic rights and social services are provided only to keep the population quiescent. To complicate matters still further, some people within a government may actually try to use it for the good of all, while others may seek to perpetuate the power and wealth of the few. Or some within government may deceive themselves into thinking that they are acting for the good of all, while in fact their policies always benefit some subgroup within a ruling class. In cases like these, it will be difficult to tell whether the cynical hypothesis is correct or not.

In these ambiguous situations, it will be unclear to citizens whether the government is their friend or their foe and thus whether they do or do not have an obligation to support governmental institutions.

Whether or not people have an obligation to support the institutions of government, they may nonetheless have other political obligations. If a government—either through design or through innocent causes—harms its citizens or fails to treat them well, we may have obligations to our fellow citizens to try to improve things. Even if we have no obligation to the government itself, it does not follow that we should only look out for ourselves. If we have a general obligation to be concerned for the well-being of those around us and if their lives are worsened by government policies, we may have a duty to try to change the government and its policies. Likewise, if we ourselves are unjustly harmed by these policies, we have a right to try to alter them in order to protect our own interests.

These are important points because they make it clear that there can be political obligations that are not obligations to the government. Rather, they are obligations to other people who live under the same government we do. While some cynics will simply look out for themselves, this is not the only possible response to the facts that cynicism highlights. Other responses are at least as rational and are better from a moral point of view.

These points suggest yet another flaw in Socrates' benefit argument. Suppose that a person is a member of the favored class that a government acts for. She benefits greatly from its policies, while others suffer. Indeed, the suffering of others makes possible the benefits she receives. In this case, although the citizen benefits, she is not obligated to support the government. Rather, she is the recipient of unjust benefits and privileges. Though the government benefits her, she has no moral obligation to support it because it is unjust. This is not to deny that she has reasons of self-interest to perpetuate the government, but she is not morally obligated to do so. Indeed, she may be morally obligated to attempt to change it, even though this will result in her loss of special benefits and privileges.

The Lessons of Cynicism

Cynicism makes clear that the automatic and complete obedience super patriots advocate is not always appropriate. We need to know something about a government and its policies before we can determine that we have any obligations to it. Cynicism makes clear that governments might not be a force for good, and a little knowledge of history supports the view that many governments have not been. These facts are clearly relevant to our ideas about the obligations we have to support and obey government institutions.

As I have already noted, however, even if cynicism is true, that does not mean political obligations are nonexistent. Some cynics see the flaws of government and believe that they have a moral duty to change and improve things. They become reformers, trying to improve their government and make it serve people's interests. While they recognize no obligations to the government itself, they feel an obligation to their fellow citizens, and this is what motivates their efforts to bring about an improvement in the government.

In addition, while cynics deny that we are obligated to support governments or obey laws, they make it clear that our lack of obligation results from the nature of the goverment. It is because governments are exploitative that citizens have no obligation to support them. Even though this is a negative view, it does suggest a positive ideal as well. If there were a government that was genuinely dedicated to working for justice and the common good, then citizens might well be obligated to support it and obey its laws. Underlying the cynic's view, then, is a criterion that a government might be able to satisfy and a suggestion about the conditions under which political obligations could exist.

Some people reject the possibility of such a government, however, and they are led from cynicism to anarchism. They believe that governments cannot be improved. For them, the only improvement would be the dissolution of government entirely. If government is necessarily harmful to the interests of most people, then anarchism becomes an ideal that is at least worth considering. Anarchism, then, is one of the possible implications of cynicism, although (as we will see) there are other bases for anarchism as well.

In any case, it is time to look at this extreme anti-government position. For, if anarchists are right, the belief that there is a duty to obey the law and to support governmental institutions is always a mistake.

Notes

1. Wolff, *In Defense of Anarchism,* 113.
2. For Lenin's discussion, see Lenin, "State and Revolution," chap. 1, 381–395.

3. For his description of life in a utopian Communist society, see ibid., chap. 5, part 4, 417–423.

4. For Gandhi's views, see M. K. Gandhi, *Non-Violent Resistance* (New York: Shocken Books, 1961), especially sections 1 and 3.

The Case for Anarchism

ANARCHISM IS THE VIEW THAT GOVERNMENT OFFICIALS HAVE NO moral right to the powers they possess, that individuals have no moral duty to obey the government or its laws, and that governments ought to be abolished. From an anarchist point of view, governmental authority is always illegitimate and should not exist.

Anarchism may seem to be so unrealistic that it is not even worth considering. Governments are so powerful and so well entrenched that the idea of their actually being abolished is virtually beyond belief. Nonetheless, if we are trying to form our own attitude toward government, it is important to consider the anarchist challenge.

If anarchists could convince us that governments are illegitimate, then even if we could find no way to do away with them, our attitude toward governments might be one of resignation rather than support or respect. So how we think of ourselves and our duties as citizens will be profoundly affected by our response to the anarchist challenge. As anarchists or cynics, we may resign ourselves to living within the rules set down by governments because we have no choice. This will be very different, however, from the attitudes we will have if we come to decide that some governments are good, necessary, and worthy of our support.

Anarchism is, in fact, very important for anyone who thinks generally about political institutions. Whether governments should exist at all is perhaps *the* fundamental question of political philosophy. If one can show why anarchists are wrong to reject government entirely, that will provide a way of understanding how governmental power can be legitimate and why there might be a moral obligation to obey laws.

In considering anarchism, I will focus on three arguments that are at the heart of the anarchist view. They express what I think are the main reasons that have made anarchism an attractive view.

The Argument from Freedom and Autonomy

One of the central arguments for anarchism begins by appealing to the extreme value of freedom and the importance of autonomy to every individual. If freedom is the most important thing that exists and if governments by their nature limit people's freedom, then governments are essentially destructive of what has the highest value. Likewise, if freedom is something of such great value, then no individual should give up freedom by recognizing a government as having legitimate power over him.

This argument focuses on two things: (1) the idea that individual freedom or autonomy has extraordinary value and (2) the idea that governments and laws necessarily limit freedom by imposing restrictions on individuals and supporting these restrictions with force.

A first question that arises for anarchists concerns the great value they attach to freedom. Why is freedom so valuable or important? Anarchists can give a plausible answer to this question, however, because most of us do value freedom, both as a personal value and as a political value. Patrick Henry has been remembered for over two hundred years because of the stirring words he spoke about freedom before the American Revolution. He began by asking, "Is life so dear or peace so sweet as to be purchased at the price of chains and slavery?" And he answered, "I know not what course others may take, but as for me, give me liberty, or give me death!"

What Henry was saying is that freedom has a greater value than either life or peace, and therefore, if he were forced to make a choice between a peaceful life in chains or no life at all, he would choose no life at all. Death is preferable to loss of liberty.

Many of us would probably be less bold in asserting that we would risk death for liberty, but there are good reasons why everyone places a high value on freedom. This high value follows from two facts. First, all of us value and desire many things. Second, freedom is simply the ability to act to achieve our goals and satisfy our desires. So anyone who wants anything at all will want the freedom to try to obtain it.[1] This explains why the loss of freedom is much more significant than the loss of other individual goods. If we lose our freedom, we will be unable to try to achieve many goals and satisfy many desires. Freedom, then, is a very important good because it is necessary for obtaining many of the other goods that we want. It is no wonder, then, that people value freedom, and anarchists are in a strong position when they appeal to the value of freedom in justifying their anti-government view.

We can reach the same conclusion by starting with the idea of coercion. As we saw earlier, coercive powers are essential to governments. The threat of coercion that lies behind a law is what differentiates a law from a request or recommendation. Coercion, however, involves forcing someone to do what they do not want to do. For this reason, it is no surprise that coercion is something none of us wants to experience. If being coerced is being forced to do what you do not want to do, then no one wants to be coerced—because everyone wants to do what he or she wants to do. If governments are necessarily coercive and if coercion is an evil that no one wants to be subject to, then no one should want to be subject to coercion by government.

This argument about coercion is the flip side of the appeal to freedom. If freedom is a positive value and coercion deprives people of freedom, then coercion is an evil. Therefore, if we value our freedom and do not want to be coerced, we will oppose the setting up of governments that have the power to coerce us and to limit our freedom.

Robert Paul Wolff puts forward a variation of the argument from freedom and autonomy in his book *In Defense of Anarchism.*[2] Wolff argues that if governments are legitimate, then they have a right to issue laws or commands and people have a moral duty to obey these commands. However, Wolff says, every person is morally responsible for his own actions and has a moral duty to take full responsibility for what he does. In order to do this, each of us must act autonomously. We must be ruled and directed by ourselves and by our own ideas of what we take to be the right thing to do. Essentially, for Wolff, people have an obligation to make up their own minds about what is the best thing to do and then to act on that judgment. In fact, Wolff believes that this is the supreme moral obligation people have. His view is similar to one expressed by Thoreau when he wrote: "The only obligation which I have a right to assume, is to do at any time what I think right."[3]

Governments, however, claim that they have a right to tell us what to do, irrespective of what we think is best. Therefore, there is an unavoidable conflict between governmental authority and individual autonomy. One rules out the other, and so we must choose between them. Wolff, believing that the preservation of moral autonomy is our primary duty, rejects the idea that governments have legitimate authority and thus embraces the anarchist philosophy.

This is essentially the same argument that we have been considering, except that Wolff focuses on moral autonomy rather than freedom generally. In addition, he claims not only that freedom is an important value but that all of us have a duty to preserve our freedom to act on our own beliefs. For him, then, anarchism has its foundation not only in our deep preference for liberty but also in a moral obligation that we have to preserve our autonomy. For Wolff, giving up liberty is not only foolish, it is immoral.

The Argument from the Evil of Coercing Others

The argument from freedom and autonomy that I have described is, in a certain sense, self-centered. It urges us to take seriously our own freedom and to resist government because it encroaches on our own autonomy. Similar objections to government arise, however, if we take seriously the autonomy of other people and think that there is a duty to respect their autonomy. A person may accept anarchism not simply because she does not want to be coerced herself. She may also believe that it is wrong to coerce others, especially by means of threats or the application of force and violence.[4]

This argument can be seen as a generalization of those we have considered already. If freedom and autonomy are so valuable that I ought not to compromise *my* freedom or autonomy by recognizing a government that limits them, then I also ought not to recognize government authority because it limits the freedom and autonomy of *others* as well.

This argument can also arise from a belief in the ideal of equality. If all people have equal rights and if all people are, in some sense, of equal value, then it is wrong for some people to have power over others. It is wrong for some to exercise authority or to threaten punishments or to impose punishments as a means of bringing about obedience to the law. All of these actions that are typical of governments are violations of people's rights to live according to their own judgment of what is best.

The argument can be related as well to Immanuel Kant's famous principle that in all our actions, we should "treat humanity . . . always at the same time as an end and never simply as a means."[5] That is, we should always recognize that people are ends in themselves that possess intrinsic value, that the value of people should never be thought of solely in terms of their usefulness to others. Yet, if we interfere with a person's acting on his best assessment of how to behave, then we are relegating his goals and ideals to a lower status than that of other people. We are coercing him so that others may benefit. This, the anarchist can argue, is to treat him simply as a means.

One might object to the anarchist that this argument overlooks the fact that people cannot help but affect one another by their actions. We are not purely isolated beings. What we do affects others, and therefore we need to coordinate our actions so that we can prosper and avoid harm.

Anarchists can agree to all these points. What they insist on, however, is that the cooperation that is required between human beings can be and should be obtained by voluntary agreements and not by coercion. Anarchists do not object to the goal of coordinating people's activities in mutually beneficial ways. What they object to is the use of force and coercion as means to achieve this goal. As we have seen earlier, however, force and coercion are essential to government, and that is why anarchists oppose government.

In opposing governments, then, anarchists do not deny that our actions affect one another, and they do not deny the need to coordinate our actions so as to avoid harm to one another. Anarchists believe that it is possible to achieve these goals through voluntary cooperation among people. Any other means of attaining cooperation will violate the autonomy and individuality of other human beings. In the words of the anarchist writer Peter Kropotkin:

> We . . . foresee a state of society where the liberty of the individual will be limited by no laws, no bonds—by nothing else but his own social habits and the necessity, which everyone feels, of finding cooperation, support, and sympathy among his neighbors.[6]

So anarchists are not ignorant of the need for cooperation, but they believe it can be achieved without the coercive activities of government.

The Evils of Governments

There is a final argument for anarchism that draws on many of the points made by political cynics. If governments are institutions that exercise coercion over most people in order to benefit a few, then their effects on most people will be harmful. The centralization of power that one finds in governments leads to abuses of people and thus to the creation of widespread misery. If the concentrated power of government did not exist, then small groups of people would not be able to dominate the rest of the society, and life could be much better for most people.[7]

This is not to say that if there were no governments, all would be perfect. Anarchists need not believe that a perfect, utopian life is possible. Nonetheless, they are committed to the view that governments make things worse and thus that doing away with governments would improve the lives of most people.

In making their case, anarchists often point to three aspects of political society that they believe generate much misery. First, while some anarchists have advocated capitalism as the economic system that maximizes human freedom, others have been strongly opposed to capitalism and private property.[8] These anti-capitalist anarchists argue that the institutions of the state are used to protect the ability of small numbers of individuals to accumulate goods and wealth, while others who are in need do not have enough. If the law protects property rights, this means that the force of the state will be used to keep people who are poor from having their needs met. At the same time, those who have accumulated a great surplus can count on armies and police to stand guard for them and to protect their property. As the words of one song of protest describe the situation, "The banks are made of marble, with a guard at every door, and the vaults are stuffed with silver that the people sweated for."[9] By protecting the "vaults of silver" while people go hungry, the government increases the misery that arises from imbalances in the distribution of goods.

A second institution that anarchists attack is the prison system. If we want to see whether governments are on the whole beneficial or harmful, we need to consider the fact that in enforcing the law, governments inflict harsh punishments on people. People who violate the law are deprived of their liberty and required to spend significant portions of their lives in confinement and discomfort. The misery created by the use of imprisonment and other punishments needs to be taken into account in any assessment of the overall effects of government. This is especially so if people are imprisoned for theft and if the system of private property is itself unjust. According to this view, the people suffering in prison are being punished for trying to meet their own needs by taking goods from others who possess them but in fact have no right to them.[10]

Finally, governments are associated with war, an activity that has generated massive destruction throughout history. Even if conflict would occur in a world without governments, it is hard to believe that the scale and intensity of conflict could be as great as it is in our world. Governments possess vast organizational powers. They can call on large numbers of people, acquire vast resources through taxation, and organize huge, effective armies to fight in far-flung places of combat. Likewise, they can draw on human and financial resources to develop weapons that small groups of individuals could never have devised on their own.[11]

So, anarchists claim, if we try to imagine a world without government and compare it with the governmentally organized world we live in, we will be led to the conclusion that government has done more harm than good. We can see this by reminding ourselves that, as cynics show, many governments actively pursue the well-being of the few and sacrifice that of the many. Moreover, even governments that pursue lofty ideals have become involved in wars of ever increasing horror. While anarchists may concede that a world without government is difficult for most of us to imagine, they are sure it would be a better world.

Notes

1. John Rawls uses the term *primary goods* to refer to those "things which it is supposed a rational man wants whatever else he wants." See John Rawls, *A Theory of Justice* (Cambridge: Harvard University Press, 1971), 92.

2. See Wolff, *In Defense of Anarchism,* 3–19 *passim.*
3. Henry David Thoreau, "Civil Disobedience," in *Walden and Other Writings of Henry David Thoreau,* ed. B. Atkinson (New York: Random House Modern Library, 1937), 637.
4. This motivation seems to underlie much of what William Lloyd Garrison asserts in his "Declaration of Sentiments, 1838," in *Nonviolence in America: A Documentary History,* ed. S. Lynd (Indianapolis: Bobbs-Merrill, 1966), 25–31.
5. Immanuel Kant, *Grounding for the Metaphysics of Morals,* trans. J. Ellington (Indianapolis: Hackett, 1981), 36.
6. Peter Kropotkin, "Anarchist Communism: Its Basis and Principles," in *Kropotkin's Revolutionary Pamphlets,* ed. Roger Baldwin (New York: Dover, 1970), 63.
7. For a statement of this argument, see Kropotkin, "Law and Authority," *Revolutionary Pamphlets,* 196–218.
8. For an example of a pro-capitalist anarchist, see David Friedman, *The Machinery of Freedom* (New York: Harper & Row, 1973). Peter Kropotkin, "Law and Authority," *Revolutionary Pamphlets,* 196–218, defends the anti-capitalist version of anarchism.
9. Les Rice, "The Banks of Marble," in *Carry It On!—A History in Song and Pictures of the Working Men and Women of America,* eds. Pete Seeger and Bob Reiser, (New York: Simon & Schuster, 1985), 178–179. Copyright Storm King Music, 1950.
10. On prisons and the problem of crime generally, see Kropotkin, "Prisons and Their Moral Influence on Prisoners," *Revolutionary Pamphlets,* 219–235.
11. Leo Tolstoy argues for the connections between governments and war in "On Patriotism" and "Patriotism, or Peace?" both of which are reprinted in *Tolstoy's Writings on Civil Disobedience and Nonviolence* (New York: New American Library, 1968).

The Case Against Anarchism

ANARCHISM IS OFTEN DISMISSED AS A FOOLISH, VISIONARY, OR utopian view, but it is nonetheless both powerful and provocative. It appeals to deep and important values like personal autonomy and respect for others, while drawing attention to the many ways in which the existence of government has been detrimental to human well-being. Having looked at some of the central arguments for anarchism, it is time to consider how defenders of government legitimacy might reply to these arguments and try to justify the legitimacy of government authority.

Hobbes and the Defense
of Government

The first argument for anarchism was based on the extreme value of freedom and personal autonomy. According to this argument, governments are illegitimate and undesirable because the existence of government necessarily results in the limiting of human freedom.

In trying to refute this argument, a person could try to show that freedom is not valuable. This is not a promising strategy, however, because freedom does seem to be very valuable, and it is strongly desired by almost all people. A more promising approach arises from the idea that even if freedom is very valuable, there are other things of value too, and it may be necessary to sacrifice some of our freedom in order to protect other things we value.

This is, in general outline, the kind of argument Thomas Hobbes develops in his book *Leviathan.* Hobbes begins his discussion of government by taking seriously the view that there should be no government and trying to show that it is mistaken.[1] Hobbes calls the situation in which no government exists "the state of nature," and he uses the term "civil society" to refer to a condition where there are governmental institutions. He then describes what life in the state of nature would be like. His aim is to show that even though it is a situation of total freedom, it is not a condition in which anyone would want to live.

Government is legitimate, according to Hobbes, because living under a government is better than living in the state of nature. The advantages of government are so great that it is worth sacrificing some of our freedom in order to bring about these advantages. For this reason, rational people would consent to sign a social contract and subject themselves to the laws and powers of a government. Government is legitimate because if people

70

were offered a choice between government and anarchy and if they understood what living in a state of nature would actually be like, they would agree to have a government.

Hobbes agrees with the anarchist that if there were no government, there would be no coercion by laws, and everyone would have the freedom to do whatever he likes. Unlike the anarchist, Hobbes does not find this an attractive situation. Even though as individuals each of us might want total freedom, Hobbes does not think that we would be comfortable with everyone else having this same amount of freedom.

Why not? Because in the state of nature, conflict between people is inevitable, and no one can be confident that he will do well in this state of conflict. Everyone is vulnerable to death, injury, and other losses at the hands of other people. The state of nature, Hobbes tells us, would be a "war of all against all," and human life would be "solitary, poor, nasty, brutish, and short."[2] It would be so terrible that any rational person would be willing to give up some portion of his freedom in order to increase his security. Any rational person would be willing to trade away some freedom (for example, his own freedom to kill or injure others) if others would agree to do the same. If everyone gives up some freedom, then everyone ends up more secure.

What Hobbes describes, then, is a situation in which everyone is totally free, but they come to realize that they would be better off if they had less freedom. Because no one is free from attack in the state of nature, all are willing to sign a social contract, pledging to give up their freedom if others do the same. They create government as the mechanism for enforcing the limitations that they accept in the contract. A mere promise not to attack others is not, according to Hobbes, sufficient to ensure compliance with the contract. Enforcement by the threat and imposition of punishment is necessary because, as Hobbes says, "covenants without the sword are but words."[3] The coercion that governments exercise is legitimate because people would agree to it as a necessary means of escaping from the conditions of life in a state of nature.

Is Hobbes Too Pessimistic?

One might think that Hobbes is too negative in his view of human nature and too pessimistic about life without government. On first reading Hobbes, many people think he is claiming that people are inherently evil and that it is the moral flaws in people that lead to conflict and the war of all against all. Others think that Hobbes sees human beings as totally selfish, concerned only about their own interests and not at all about others.

In my view, Hobbes's argument does not depend on these sorts of negative assumptions about human nature. If it did depend on these assumptions, Hobbes's argument would not be as powerful as it is. In fact, of course, people are capable of caring about one another and are capable of acting morally. These facts do not undermine Hobbes's argument. The reason for this is that the extreme conflicts of the state of nature do not grow out of defects of human nature. Rather, they grow out of a combination of facts about human beings and about the situation people find themselves in. Given certain facts about the world, conflict would arise even if people were quite unselfish.

The first source of conflict in the state of nature is the scarcity of resources. People are forced into competition with one another because they find themselves in a world in which they need the same things in order to survive and to enjoy life. As Hobbes says,

> [If] any two men desire the same thing, which never-theless they cannot both enjoy, they become enemies; and in the way to their end, (which is principally their

> own conservation, and sometimes their delectation
> only,) endeavor to destroy, or subdue one another.[4]

All people have the goal of survival ("their own conserva-
tion") and desire a pleasant rather than a difficult life.
Given these goals and desires, people have a need for
the same food, shelter, and other goods, and one
person's possession of these often results in another's
lacking them. Hence, people are in competition for the
goods required for life.

In addition, because people recognize that they are
in competition with one another for life's necessities,
they come to see that they threaten one another, and
this provides them with another motive for conflict. This
is the motive of fear or suspicion that Hobbes calls "diffi-
dence." One person (A) might attack another (B) not to
gain B's goods but rather to prevent B from attacking A.
This motive is essentially the logic behind preemptive
attacks and the idea that "the best defense is a good
offense."

This is a quite rational motive, but it tends to increase the amount and ferocity of competition. Indeed,
since everyone is a threat to everyone else, all have a
motive to attack others. Even if a person did not want to
take part in this process, he would be caught up in it
simply because he wants to survive. No "bad" motives are
necessary. Any person who wants to survive and under-
stands the conflicts of interest between himself and others would come to be fearful and mistrusting of others.
In a world of scarcity and unlimited freedom, every person would regard every other person's existence as a
threat to his own life and well-being.

Finally, Hobbes points out that some people do simply like to dominate others, that they are impelled to
conflict by the desire for glory, the desire to be "top dog"
or "number one." This desire is obviously a source of
conflict because only one person can enjoy this status.
This motive provides the person on top with a reason to

perpetuate his domination, but it provides others with a motive to change things and set themselves up as the dominant person.

The situation might stabilize if some people could achieve dominance. According to Hobbes, however, this is impossible. "Nature hath made men so equal, in the faculties of body and mind," he says, that no person possesses the strength or intelligence to assure victory in competition with others.[5] There are differences among people, but the differences are not great enough to assure anyone success. Even if one person is stronger than others, she is vulnerable to attack by weaker people who join together or who use intelligence and trickery to trap her. The implication of human equality for Hobbes is that all people are vulnerable to attack. All men and women are mortal. No one is invincible.

The result of all of these facts is that life in the state of nature would be intolerable. Each of us would be surrounded by enemies and constantly subject to attacks that could lead to death or injury. Moreover, there would be no reason to try to make our lives better through cultivation of land or production of goods. A person who produces things of value simply makes himself into a more attractive target for attack. His possession of valuable things gives people an additional incentive to attack him. This is why Hobbes says that life in the state of nature would be a life of continual fear and that none of the benefits of civilization could be enjoyed.[6]

The Benefits of Civil Society

Suppose that it were possible to transform the state of nature into civil society. In this case, there would be a government and a system of laws that would apply to everyone. The government would have the right to create whatever laws are necessary for producing social peace and the power to enforce these laws. Violators would be prosecuted and punished.

In this condition, everyone would be less free than in the state of nature. They could no longer act in ways that were permitted in the state of nature. In addition, however, everyone would be much more secure. Individuals would know that if they attacked others in order to obtain their goods or out of suspicion or the desire for glory, the government would forcibly prevent the attack or impose a punishment afterward. Each person would fear being punished and would therefore refrain from attacking others. For this reason, people would no longer fear being the victims of such attacks by others.

If Hobbes is right that civil society would be a situation in which people would enjoy peace and security, then he has a powerful objection to the anarchist's argument from freedom and autonomy. He does not deny that freedom and autonomy are of great value. Nor does he deny that in an ideal world a person might want the maximum amount of freedom available. He asks us, however, to consider the implications of everyone's possessing this amount of freedom, and he points out that if everyone possessed total freedom, then everyone would be badly off.

The first thing that follows from Hobbes's argument is that under certain conditions, it is rational to give up some of our freedom and autonomy. It is rational because freedom is not the only value. Security from attack is also an important value, and if we need to give up some of our freedom in order to be secure, then that is a worthwhile bargain to strike.

The second thing Hobbes's argument shows is that government can be desirable and legitimate. Government is desirable because it enforces the limitations on people's freedom that create security for all. Government is legitimate because it is something people would consent to if they think through the implications of living without government in the state of nature. Since people would consent to a government if they were offered a choice, then the government's claim to its powers is neither arbitrary nor contrary to people's desires.

The upshot of this discussion of Hobbes is that he makes a strong case against the first anarchist argument, the appeal to freedom and autonomy. He refutes this argument by showing that there are good reasons why rational people would give up some of their autonomy. The primary one, according to Hobbes, is the desire to live in peace and security. If that can only be satisfied under a government, then all of us have a powerful reason to approve of, consent to, and support governmental institutions.

The Legitimacy of Coercion

The second argument for anarchism rests on the view that by coercing people, governments fail to accord proper respect to people as autonomous beings who are ends in themselves. This argument is not convincing, however.

Let us grant that we ought to respect other human beings as autonomous agents who possess intrinsic worth. Nonetheless, we know that people can decide to act in ways that are threatening to ourselves or others. If someone wants to kill or injure me, then the carrying out of his autonomous actions will interfere with my ability to carry out my autonomous actions. Moreover, his attacking me (for pleasure or gain) will treat me as a means to his goals, thus violating the very principle of respect to persons that the anarchist appeals to. So permitting him to attack as he wishes in order to respect *his* autonomy results in allowing me to be treated in a way that violates *my* autonomy. Inevitably, in this sort of case, someone's autonomy is violated.[7]

Or suppose it is not I but some other person who is the object of attack. The same problem arises. One person's autonomous choice will lead to interference with another's. In this case, not everyone can have his way. Someone is going to be a victim of interference. There is a widespread moral consensus that in this type of situation it is legitimate to use force to prohibit one person from attacking another and violating his rights. It is better to violate the autonomy of the attacker than to permit the violation of the victim's autonomy.

To use force in order to prevent this kind of attack does not violate the attacker's rights or her worth as a person, for no one has a right to initiate this kind of attack. Coercion can be morally legitimate in those cases where it is used to prevent someone from doing something she has no right to do. In such cases, the person being coerced will not like it, but the coercion is legitimate because it is not a violation of anyone's rights.

Like Hobbes's argument, this argument appeals to the fact that freedom is not the only thing of value. Life and security from injury are important values as well. When these conflict, it is sometimes more important to protect people from death and injury than it is to guarantee freedom and autonomy to all. This is clearly implied in the common belief that it is permissible to kill someone in self-defense or in defense of others' lives. To have a right of self-defense is to have a right to interfere with the freedom and autonomy of the person who is threatening one's life. It is to have a right to use force and coercion in defense of one's own right to life.[8]

We can extend this further. If I have a right to use coercion to defend my life and physical well-being, then it is plausible to infer that I have a right to delegate this task to someone else. I could, for example, hire a bodyguard if I thought this person could defend me better than I could defend myself. (In delegating this authority, however, I need to be sure that the bodyguard will carry out his job in a responsible way that respects the rights of others.)

Likewise, a community of people, each of whom possesses a right of self-defense, could hire a few people to serve as police officers, people whose sole task it is to provide protection for members of the community. This action could be defended as a more efficient means of doing what each person has an individual right to do, defend his or her life. As soon as people begin to delegate these tasks, however, they have begun to set up the very sort of protective institution that Hobbes claims constitutes a government.[9]

Anarchists will argue, of course, that it is illegitimate to set up government institutions like this. The argument against their view is quite plausible, however. If it is legitimate to defend oneself or others from attack (which seems plausible) and if it is legitimate to delegate such defense to designated people (as also seems plausible), then it is legitimate to set up a special institution whose function it is to protect people from attack. Just as the defense of our lives and the lives of others gives us a justification for overriding the autonomy of attackers, it also gives a moral justification to the creation of government institutions that function to "provide for the common defense."

The second argument for anarchism is mistaken, then, because it assumes that it is always wrong to override individual autonomy by applying coercion. The argument we have just considered, however, shows that overriding the autonomy of others and applying coercive measures to them can sometimes be morally justified. If governments apply coercion in these justified cases, then that use of coercion by governments can be justified as well. Therefore, government coercion can be legitimate.

The Benefits of Government

In replying to the first two arguments for anarchism, I have tried to show that it is possible for government to be legitimate. In principle, there is nothing wrong with giving up some of our liberty for security and nothing wrong with applying coercion to people under certain circumstances.

Hobbes goes further than this. He does not want to argue that government is legitimate in principle. He wants to argue that government is in fact legitimate and that any rational person would always prefer life under a government to life in the state of nature. That is one reason why he portrays the state of nature as such a terrible condition. In his opinion, any government is better than no government.

As we have seen, however, anarchists claim that the evils of government outweigh the evils of the state of nature. They think that governments create more human misery than would exist without them. Cynics, likewise, argue that governments benefit the few who hold power, using the resources of the many for the sake of the rulers themselves. That is the third argument for anarchism: that governments do more harm than good, that most people would be better off without them.

If anarchists could prove that governments do more harm than good, then their case would be made. For even if governments could in principle be legitimate if they provide security and use coercion to protect people's rights, that does not show that actual governments are legitimate. It only shows that governments are legitimate *if* they carry out these functions. If actual governments do not carry out these functions but instead are themselves a threat to people's well-being, then actual governments are not legitimate.

Hobbes's defense of actual governments rests on two related claims: First, that any person would prefer a government to the state of nature, and second, that having a government is in everyone's mutual interest.

The first of these claims is based on the idea that in the state of nature virtually everyone is my enemy. For this reason, I have to fear attack from all sides. Under a government, however, I can have at least partial security. This is why Hobbes thought one would necessarily be better off under a system of government.

What this Hobbesian argument overlooks, however, is that in civil society, the government may be my enemy, and the well-organized enmity of the government may be much more dangerous than the diffused enmity of many different people. It is hard to believe, for example, that Jews or resistance leaders pursued by the Gestapo under Nazi rule were better off than they would have been in the state of nature. In the state of nature, an individual has an equal chance against other individuals, but these chances are much diminished when the enemy is a vast organization that has widespread powers and large resources.

Against Hobbes, then, I would argue that anyone would prefer to take his chances in the state of nature rather than to have to contend with organized pursuit. Hobbes seems to be mistaken in his belief that it is always rational for individuals to opt for civil society rather than the state of nature. He assumes that the state of nature is the worst of all possible worlds, but reflection on the powers of totalitarian regimes shows this to be false.

One might think that even if there are some individuals who are more harmed than helped by government, nonetheless, for people generally, government has represented a great advance, that humanity generally has been and remains better off with governments than it would be without them. This view, however, like the opposite view held by the anarchist, is difficult to verify.

We can look at governments as institutions that have taken great steps to tame the conflicts that exist between individuals and to bring the benefits of coordination and cooperation to large numbers of people. Through laws and court systems, governments have provided a context in which people could settle disputes without violence. Likewise, through centralizing some resources, governments are able to provide assistance to people in need and to aid the victims of floods, epidemics, food shortages, and other natural disasters. There is no doubt that these benefits have been produced and that they probably would not have been produced without governments.

Yet many governments have been tyrannical and have simply centralized the powers to victimize, brutalize, and plunder. Moreover, even the respectable motive of self-defense has led to the development of huge arsenals of nuclear weapons, chemical weapons, biological weapons, and other explosives. These weapons have the potential to destroy all of human life. If human beings end up destroying themselves with such weapons, that will provide a decisive refutation of Hobbes's view that civil society is better than the state of nature. It will show (though no one will be around to realize it) that anarchists were right in thinking that humanity would have been better off if governments had never come into existence.

We do not know whether or not this will happen, and for this reason we are not in a position to state with confidence that the overall effects of government have been or will be primarily good or primarily evil. The verdict on the argument from the good and bad effects of government is still out.

What Hobbes Has Shown

What Hobbes does succeed in showing is that there are deep difficulties in claiming unlimited freedom for ourselves or granting it to others. He shows how it can be legitimate to give up some of our freedom and to limit the freedom of others in the interests of survival and other important values. He makes a plausible case that we would accept institutions with coercive powers in order to protect ourselves and others from attack.

Nonetheless, as we have seen, these arguments do not provide a blanket approval of every government that exists. At best, they provide an approval of governments that actually protect people and that increase their security. Hobbes shows that legitimate governments are possible. Insofar as these governments carry out their protective role properly, they will be worthy of our support, and we will have reason to obey their laws. Moreover, if we or others choose not to obey, these governments will have the power to enforce the laws through punishment or other means.

What Hobbes cannot show is that all governments actually carry out these protective functions. No abstract argument or theory could possibly show this. Thus, he cannot prove that every government—or indeed any particular one—is worthy of our support. This can only be determined by looking at the actual government—what aims it seeks to achieve, what policies it seeks to enforce, and what methods it uses.

Hobbes does provide an answer to anarchism, however, in the sense that he shows how we could approve of an institution that exercises coercive powers over ourselves and others. To this extent, he succeeds in making the case for the desirability and legitimacy of government.

There is one final objection, however, that I have not considered, and that is Robert Paul Wolff's argument about the inconsistency between governmental authority and moral autonomy. If our primary obligation is to maintain our right and ability to make moral choices and to act according to them, then perhaps it is morally wrong to trade our autonomy for increased security. Even if it is expedient to do this, we may have a moral duty not to.

Suppose, however, that we can both recognize the legitimacy of government and retain our moral autonomy. If this is possible, then we need not make the choice that Wolff describes. This possibility is precisely what is claimed by proponents of what I have called critical citizenship. It is time to take a closer look at this approach.

Notes

1. Thomas Hobbes's *Leviathan* was originally published in 1651. The basic argument that I summarize can be found in Chapters 13, 14, and 17.
2. Ibid., chap.13, 104.
3. Ibid., chap.17, 138.
4. Ibid., chap.13, 102.
5. Ibid., chap.13, 101.
6. Not everyone agrees with Hobbes's conception of what life would be like without government. For two classic dissents,

see John Locke's *Two Treatises on Civil Government* and Rousseau's *Discourse on the Origins of Inequality*. For a more recent discussion, see Robert Axelrod, *The Evolution of Cooperation* (New York: Basic Books, 1984).

7. Robert Dahl makes a similar argument against anarchism in *Democracy and Its Critics* (New Haven, CT: Yale University Press, 1990), 45.

8. This view of the right to self-defense is put forward in Jan Narveson, "Pacifism: A Philosophical Analysis," *Ethics* 75 (1965), 259–271.

9. Robert Nozick puts forward this sort of argument in *Anarchy, State, and Utopia* (New York: Basic Books, 1973), 12.

CHAPTER 6

Critical Citizenship

CRITICAL CITIZENSHIP IS THE VIEW THAT WHETHER ONE OUGHT to support a government and whether one has a moral obligation to obey the law depends on the nature of the particular government and the nature of the law in question. For the advocate of critical citizenship, the answer to the question of whether political obligations exist is, "It all depends." As we saw in Chapter 1, Martin Luther King expressed this view when he argued that while people have an obligation to obey just laws, they have a right—and perhaps even a duty—to disobey unjust laws. The duty to obey depends on the nature of the law.[1]

Critical citizenship is a plausible ideal. It takes account of a fact that has already been prominent in our discussion. Governments have the potential both to make us safer and better off and also to abuse and exploit us. They can be operated for the common good or for the good of a privileged group. For this reason, it is implausible to think that all governments are owed the same degree of allegiance, no matter what those in power are aiming to do and no matter what effect they actually have on people's lives.

Yet this is just what both anarchists and super patriots claim. Anarchists claim that we have no obligation to any governments or laws, no matter how good they are. Super patriots claim that we have a deep obligation to our own government and its laws, no matter how bad they are. Critical citizens reject the all-or-nothing perspective that anarchists and super patriots have in common.

Objections to
Critical Citizenship

The ideal of critical citizenship comes under attack from two sides. Anarchists complain that critical citizens are wrong to take government and law seriously at all. According to them, citizens should behave autonomously, deciding for themselves what is best to do and doing what they think is best. Since critical citizenship implies that on some occasions we should do something just because it is the law, anarchists regard this as a forfeiting of our autonomy. As we saw earlier, Robert Paul Wolff claims that this is immoral.

Super patriots also attack the ideal of critical citizenship. They believe that respect for government and law requires that we always obey the law, no matter what. They criticize critical citizenship because it says that citizens must make choices about whether to obey the law and that on some occasions citizens ought not to do what is required by law. From the super patriotic perspective, this is the equivalent of anarchy. Super patriots wonder what would happen if people felt free to disobey the law whenever they disagreed with its requirements. They don't believe that a system of laws and government can exist if citizens feel that they can decide for themselves whether to be loyal or not and whether to obey or disobey.

Can these very different objections be answered by advocates of critical citizenship?

Let us turn first to Wolff's anarchist criticism, the idea that it is never right to do something just because the law requires it.[2] In effect, what this objection does is raise the question why we should take the law seriously at all. Part of the answer has already emerged in our discussion of Hobbes. The system of law may be beneficial to us, and if it is, then we have a reason to support the law by showing respect toward it and complying with its directives. This does not seem irrational. If the existence of a system of laws brings about a condition in which conflicts between people are diminished and those that exist can be handled peacefully and if our lives are better and will continue to be better because such laws exist, then we have a reason for supporting the system.

Note that this argument is, like Socrates', based on an appeal to the beneficial effects of government. Unlike Socrates' argument, however, it appeals to future benefits rather than past ones. It does not say that we should obey the law from gratitude. Rather, it says that we should obey so that we can continue to benefit from the system of laws. This argument, like Hobbes's, appeals to our own interest and tries to show why obedience is good for us.

There is a second reason for obeying the laws that is less egocentric. We may support the system of laws because it creates a better situation for people other than ourselves. The same benefits that we receive from a legal system will be received by others as well. In fact, the legal system may support and strengthen important moral ideals. As Martin Luther King wrote, "law and order exist for the purpose of establishing justice."[3] If the laws help to accomplish these goals, then a person who is concerned with justice will support the law and will seek to have others accept it as well.

How can this support be shown? Obviously, we can show our support by praising the legal system and urging others to support it. As we know, however, "talk is cheap" and "actions speak louder than words." In order to show that we take the law seriously, we must show that we are willing to order our own lives in accord with the law. We must show that we are willing to do what the law requires even when this requires some personal sacrifice or even when we think that a different law or policy might be somewhat better. It is through obedience to the system of law that we show our support for it. We show others that they should take the laws seriously by taking the laws seriously ourselves.

The Ideal of Social Cooperation

It may still be puzzling why we do this, however. Again, Hobbes's discussion is helpful. Hobbes thought of government as coming into existence in an agreement among people. Using the metaphor of a social contract, he described how people accept limits on their own behavior on the condition that others do the same. Each of us agrees, for example, to give up the right to kill or injure other people on the condition that other people give up the right to kill us. The social contract is an attempt by people to cooperate and to establish a system of peace that no one could create single-handedly.

Hobbes himself thought that the fear of punishment was the only thing that could actually make people cooperate and obey the law, and for this reason he argued for a very powerful government that could enforce the laws and deter violations through fear of punishment. Fear, however, is not the only motive for obeying the law.

As King argues, the desire for justice can also motivate obedience to law. Moreover, if we view the law as a cooperative enterprise whose purpose is to create peace and justice, then we may obey the law as a way of keeping faith with other people with whom we want to cooperate. We want others to obey on occasions when they may disagree with the law, and so we obey when we disagree. This shows our good faith and our willingness to override our own interests and desires in order to uphold the terms of social cooperation. Just as we urge others to support the law, so we too are willing to do so. We claim no special exceptions for ourselves.

While Wolff is correct to stress the value of personal autonomy, he overlooks the implications of both our need to cooperate with others and the respect we owe to others as autonomous beings. As Robert Dahl has argued, if preserving our own autonomy were the only important goal, we would have to be hermits or dictators or find people to live with who (miraculously) always want to do just what we want.[4]

Anyone who relates to others as equals, however, must sometimes defer to their wishes or judgment. Anyone who makes a promise limits her autonomy by binding herself to take certain actions in the future. Anyone who takes an oath of office, forms a friendship, enters into marriage, or has children curtails his or her own autonomy. When our entering into a relationship with others generates moral obligations, then we acquire a reason to act in accord with what these relationships require. One might say that entering into specific relationships is a way of giving our tacit consent to play by the rules that are associated with that relationship. A better way of saying this is that when we enter into relationships of various sorts with other people, our doing so gives rise to expectations about our future behavior. These expectations are based on shared understandings of the nature of the relationship. Respect for other persons should make us want to fulfill those expectations and thus provides us with a reason for taking the duties that grow out of relationships seriously.

Just as being a friend, office holder, husband, wife, or parent provides us with a reason for doing certain things, so being a citizen provides us with a reason for obeying the law. To be a citizen is to be a member of a cooperative association, and we owe the other members our obedience to the rules. We owe them the same behavior that we expect from them.

Note that in saying this, I am not supporting a forfeiture of our moral autonomy. We still retain the duty to consider our actions, and we need not put ourselves absolutely in the control of others. Moreover, we retain the duty to assess the system of which we are members and to make sure that it is a just system that does bring peace, security, and justice to other members of our society. If it does, however, then we have a duty to obey, and it is through obedience that we do our fair share to support the system.

If the system itself is evil and does not promote justice or if it abuses our rights and the rights of others, then the duty to comply with its demands is diminished or dissolved. If it ceases to be a fair system of cooperation, with others breaking their implicit promise to us, then we may have less obligation to support the system through our own actions.

Martin Luther King believed that the law was a force for justice, and he wanted white people to obey the law, even when it required them to overcome deep-seated racial prejudices. He pledged his own respect for law as a way of showing good faith in a cooperative endeavor with his fellow citizens. Even when he felt that he had to break the law, he accepted the punishment as a way of showing his continuing respect for the ideal of law. Accepting the punishment for laws he disobeyed was his way, he said, of "expressing the very highest respect for law."[5]

That King's discussion of the importance of law comes in the context of a defense of civil disobedience shows that Wolff is mistaken in his view that respect for law is inconsistent with moral autonomy. In asserting the importance of law, King does not forsake his ability to make moral judgments about the law. He retains his ability to point out with horror and condemnation that "everything that Hitler did in Germany was 'legal,'" and he goes on to say that "if I had lived in Germany during that time, I would have aided and comforted my Jewish brothers even though it was illegal."[6]

What King makes clear is that one can take the obligation to obey the law seriously while still retaining one's right and ability to make independent moral judgments about the law and while retaining one's moral right to violate the law when the law is an instrument of great evil. He makes clear that one can take seriously one's duties as a citizen without forfeiting independent judgment or moral autonomy. Contrary to Wolff, he shows that moral autonomy and respect for rightful authorities are not mutually exclusive. We need not choose between them.

The Super Patriotic Objection

In showing that the anarchists' objection is unfounded and that critical citizenship does not sacrifice autonomy, we may deepen the concerns felt by super patriots. They do not think that citizens should have the discretion to reject laws, and they equate this discretionary power with anarchism. For them, respect for authority does rule out individual choice, and they would argue that King's attitude toward the law is an invitation to anarchy. If one person can place his judgment over the collective judgment represented by the legal and political system, then everyone may do this. And if everyone reserves the right to question and disobey, then we remain in a state of anarchy.

In answering this objection, defenders of critical citizenship can proceed first by showing that there are cases in which disobedience is obviously the morally right course of action and second by showing that a recognition of this need not imply anarchy or the supremacy of individual whim.

The simplest way to show that the principle "Always obey the law" is not morally valid is to produce an example of a law that virtually everyone would agree should be violated. Suppose that a law is passed that requires parents to kill their newborn infants. None of us would think it immoral for parents to attempt to evade this law. When we hear the biblical story of Moses's mother placing him in a basket in the river in the hope that he would be found and raised among Egyptians, we do not condemn Moses' mother for this act of disobedience. It never occurs to us that it is wrong for her not to kill her child, even though her action disobeys the Pharaoh's command. If such a law existed today, we would think that parents had a right and duty to violate it and to attempt to protect their newborn children.

Others are welcome to come up with different examples, and it is quite easy to do. We simply have to imagine that some obviously and seriously immoral action is required by law. The immorality of the action must be so serious that we think it morally better to break the law than to comply with it. In his essay on civil disobedience, Thoreau expresses this view about the Fugitive Slave Law, a law that required citizens to turn over runaway slaves to the authorities so that they could be returned to their owners. Anyone who would condemn compliance with the law in this instance is committed to the view that it is sometimes morally right to break the law. Indeed, it is hard to believe that there is anyone who would not draw the line somewhere and concede that a particular law was one that he or she would feel morally justified in disobeying.

The refusal to recognize this point is perhaps related to the idea that morality consists of a set of absolute principles and that any recognition that there are legitimate exceptions to these principles is the equivalent of rejecting absolute morality. This idea is a mistake, however. A principle can be absolute in either of two senses. It can be absolute in the sense that it permits *no exceptions,* or it can be absolute in the sense that it is *absolutely binding.*

The principle "Do not kill human beings except when doing so is necessary to defend one's own life or the lives of others" is not absolute insofar as it does permit some forms of killing. It is not an exceptionless principle. Nonetheless, from the point of view of "bindingness," it is every bit as absolute as the principle "Do not kill." To believe that there are justifiable exceptions to a moral principle or that the principle builds into itself certain cases of permissible killing (or stealing, lying, etc.) is not to embrace relativism or think that morality is a matter of taste. By acknowledging that there are cases in which killing, stealing or breaking the law are morally justified, we do not undermine the importance of affirming that these actions are *typically* wrong and that those who commit them have the burden of proof in showing that they have acted rightly.

The Dangers of Advocating Disobedience

Super patriots might acknowledge this point and yet be concerned about the effects of advocating the view that everyone has a right to "second guess" the law and violate it if they see fit. Perhaps Martin Luther King was a morally conscientious person who would only violate the law for good cause, but the example of his disobedience might influence others who are less conscientious.[7] They might draw the wrong lesson from his behavior and simply decide that it is always permissible to disobey laws that one disagrees with or dislikes.

This is no doubt a danger, and that is why King and other articulate defenders of civil disobedience always try to state some general criteria for determining whether disobedience is justified. They do not simply say that disobedience is right because they disapprove of the law. After stating that one should obey just laws and disobey unjust laws, King explicitly raises the crucial question: "How does one determine when a law is just or unjust?" He goes on to provide several tests for making this determination.

First, he says, "Any law that uplifts human personality is just. Any law that degrades human personality is unjust."[9] This criterion focuses on the effects of a law, on the impact it has on people. A law that shows respect for people and seeks to increase the dignity they enjoy in society is a just law. This is what, according to King, the 1954 Supreme Court decision to desegregate schools accomplished, and that is why it should be obeyed. The laws that uphold racial segregation, however, degrade people and make it more difficult for them to be properly respected. That is what makes them unjust and worthy of being broken.

Second, he says, "An unjust law is a code that a majority inflicts on a minority that is not binding on itself."[10] As many have argued, justice requires equal and impartial treatment. Laws that support segregation, however, are passed by a majority but do not apply to the majority in the same way that they apply to the minority. The white majority did not have to attend inferior schools, use inferior eating or bathroom facilities, or live in inferior housing. If all suffered at the same level, there might be misfortune but no injustice, but given the unequally favorable treatment of one group, the laws supporting this inequality were unjust.

Third, King says, "An unjust law is a code inflicted upon a minority which that minority had no part in enacting or creating because they did not have the unhampered right to vote."[11] This criterion is a procedural one. It objects to a law because it is imposed on people who are excluded from the political process. Not only is the law imposed by a majority in a way that disadvantages a particular minority, but the minority is not permitted to take part in the political process that gives rise to the law.

Finally, King points out, "There are some instances where a law is just on its face but unjust in its application." He gives as an example a legitimate law that requires a permit to hold a parade but which is used for the purpose of depriving some citizens of "the First Amendment privilege of peaceful assembly and peaceful protest."[12] In this sort of case, a legitimate law is applied in an unjust way because it is used to curtail people's ability to exercise democratic rights that are available to others.

This list is King's attempt to differentiate justified from unjustified disobedience of laws. If his criteria are correct and if a particular case satisfies them, then it is an instance of justified disobedience to law, and a person could agree with King about this while still taking seriously the idea that in typical cases, there is a moral obligation to obey the law.

King's criteria for distinguishing just and unjust laws can be related to John Rawls's idea of the "democratic conception of society as a system of cooperation among equal persons."[13] For this ideal to be operative and relevant, citizens must be able to feel that the laws accord them the same respect and consideration that is shown to others. They must feel that the law is not more burdensome to them and beneficial to others. They must have an equal right to participate in the process that generates new laws.

If these conditions are not met, then people will be justified in viewing the laws with suspicion. Indeed, if there is anything surprising in King's letter, it is that he has any respect for law at all, given the history of legalized mistreatment of black Americans. It is not surprising that other blacks viewed the system more cynically, saw the laws as oppressive, and advocated violence as a means of achieving freedom and equality. What King seems to have believed is that, in spite of the history of legalized injustice, his best hope was to appeal to the system of law and the ideals of "equal justice under law." By expressing respect for law, King took the political and legal system at its word and tried to make it live up to its own ideals. Given the system as he describes it, it is not obvious that the legal system deserved the respect he accorded it. Nonetheless, as I noted earlier, he wanted to appeal to people's respect for law and legal ideals as a means for gaining equality for his people.

While King's criteria for determining which laws are just and unjust do not constitute a fully worked out theory, the fact that he puts them forward is important. First, his guidelines do pick out important features of the legal and political system. Second, the principles he appeals to are important and show that he is not violating the law for trivial reasons. He is not violating the law simply because he dislikes it. Nor is he violating the law for personal gain. This is especially brought out by his willingness to accept the punishment for his violation. That shows that he recognizes that the law does apply to him. He is not trying to set himself above the law or beyond its reach. Many of his actions and statements are meant to show that he supports the legal system as a whole, and in the context of this overall support they give added moral force to his decision to break the law.

What King and other spokesmen for critical citizenship must do, then, is make clear that they take the law seriously and that they are acting on general criteria that apply to all others. If others can show that their violations meet these same criteria, then advocates of critical citizenship will recognize the legitimacy of their acts. If they cannot do this, however, then their violations are wrong. The principles of the critical citizen, then, are general ones that apply to all, and they are not arbitrary or trivial.

The Morality of Obedience and Disobedience to Law

The kind of position developed by King appears to be capable of standing up to the objections raised by both anarchists and super patriots. Against anarchists, it can be shown that critical citizens do take moral autonomy and independent judgment as seriously as they ought to. Against super patriots, it can be shown that critical citizens do take their responsibility to obey the law seriously enough. Both of these points are implicitly made in King's thoughtful and eloquent "Letter from Birmingham City Jail."

There are other points King does not make but that can be used to strengthen his position. It is worth introducing some of them here in order to identify some of the issues that need to be considered in deciding when people are or are not under an obligation to obey the law. In spelling these out, I will try to show that three general questions are important: First, what sort of government is in power? Second, what sorts of procedures were followed in passing the law? Third, what sort of law is it?

Let's begin with an extreme example of the sort that political cynics stress. Suppose that a person lives under an authoritarian and tyrannical government that exists only because it has vast powers of terror and intimidation. Suppose further that the rulers make laws simply by deciding what they want to do and that they adopt a particular law simply on a whim. They just feel like having that law. Finally, suppose that the law in question is a terrible law, that it requires, for example, that citizens report anyone who is critical of the government to the police.

In this case, we would have an example of an unjust *government* that uses an arbitrary and unjust *procedure* to pass a harmful and unjust *law*. Given the evils of the government, the unfairness of the procedure for making laws, and the evil of the law itself, it is hard to believe that citizens would be morally obligated to obey such a law.

Contrast this with a case of a popularly elected government whose officials genuinely pursue justice and the well-being of their community. They follow elaborate procedures for passing laws and guarantee that no law or policy will be passed without input from knowledgeable people and concerned citizens, as well as public debate.

Finally, they pass a law that imposes a small tax that will be used to protect the quality of drinking water.

In this case, it seems obvious that citizens would have an obligation to obey the law. They have a good *government*. The government has followed a worthwhile *procedure* that gives all concerned an opportunity to participate and to have an influence on which policy is adopted. Finally, the *law* is just, reasonable, and will have a beneficial effect on the community.

A particular citizen might think that the law is not the best possible law or that the procedure could be better in certain ways or that the government is imperfect. This would not free such a person from the obligation to obey. It is not reasonable to expect perfection in laws and institutions. If they are, on the whole, just and fair and promote the public interest while respecting individual rights, then their imperfections do not justify disobedience.

Even if one is dissatisfied with the law, it remains true that a fair procedure has been used in passing it. Moreover, one has the opportunity to reraise the issue and to try to amend the policy that has been adopted. In the meantime, out of support for the system and out of respect for its success in providing a way for citizens to cooperate in solving community problems, one ought to obey the law.

In this case, we can see the limits on personal autonomy and personal judgment in operation. While I may not think the law is the best possible one, that does not justify my violating it. I ought to obey it, even if I continue to work for change.

Some of Martin Luther King's critics probably thought that this was precisely the situation he was in, and for this reason they opposed his violations of the law. Some of them probably believed that the *government* of the United States was on the whole good and just and that the *procedures* for passing laws were, on the whole, good though imperfect. They might grant that the segregation *laws* were unjust but nonetheless think that disobedience was wrong. Why? Because of the overall quality of the government and the overall goodness of political procedures. The segregation laws, according to these people, were an aberration, a flaw in a basically good system that deserved our obedience and support in spite of the injustice of the segregation laws. These people may have hoped or believed that the system would gradually improve and that the evils of racial segregation would eventually disappear.

These critics of civil disobedience might have been right if the injustice of the segregation laws and the pattern of life built on them were relatively minor. Given, however, the extreme injustice of segregation and the terrible deprivations suffered by African Americans, I think King was correct in thinking that disobedience was justified. Many people in both the federal and state governments were indifferent or hostile to black people, and many had acted to ensure that black Americans would be poorly treated and would be excluded from having a voice in the political process. But even if this were not true and even if the laws were the unintentional mistakes of good governments and good procedures, they were so seriously unjust that I believe King was correct in thinking that it was morally right for him to disobey them.

The Ideal of Critical Citizenship

The ideal of critical citizenship occupies a reasonable middle ground between the unquestioning allegiance of the super patriot and the total rejection of political obligation by the anarchist. Like the political cynic, the critical citizen believes that our obligations to support laws and governments depend on the nature and quality of those institutions. Unlike the typical cynic, however, the critical citizen does not believe that governments are all evil or unjust and that because of this no obligations exist.

For critical citizens, it is possible for governments to pass the test of decency and value, and when they do, they deserve our support. Moreover, even if they fail to pass the test fully, they may contain elements that form a basis for improvement. As we have seen, Martin Luther King could condemn many features of the American system while still valuing the Constitution, the Bill of Rights, and the rule of law. He could give them his allegiance as a way of reaching out to other citizens and urging them to make American society a more genuinely cooperative enterprise among all its citizens.

If the conclusions in this chapter are correct, then the ideal of critical citizenship is a coherent and worthwhile ideal. Moreover, it is an ideal that is more reasonable than the other outlooks we have considered. Super patriots exaggerate the allegiance we owe to laws and governments, while anarchists fail to see how citizenship could be a valuable ideal. Cynics call our attention to actual facts about government but have too simple an evaluation of the role governments play. They see only what is negative about governments, while overlooking the beneficial and worthwhile accomplishments some governments achieve.

The ideal of critical citizenship seems to get things right. People do have a moral obligation to support just laws and just institutions. We do not, however, have an obligation to support unjust laws and unjust institutions. From that, it follows that we need to think critically about the laws and institutions under which we live. Our support of them can be genuine without being uncritical and unquestioning. We need to be appreciative of the good that political systems can create, while remaining aware that not all political systems are good and that even good political systems can give rise to unjust laws and evil policies.

Notes

1. King's views are stated in his "Letter from Birmingham City Jail," 461–481.
2. Wolff, *In Defense of Anarchism,* 18.
3. King, "Letter from Birmingham City Jail," 470.
4. Dahl, *After the Revolution? Authority in a Good Society* (New Haven, CT: Yale University Press, 1970), 8–11.
5. King, "Letter from Birmingham City Jail," 469.
6. Ibid., 470.
7. An argument of this sort is put forward in Abe Fortas, *Concerning Dissent and Civil Disobedience* (New York: New American Library, 1968), 67–71.
8. King, "Letter from Birmingham City Jail," 468.
9. Ibid.
10. Ibid.
11. Ibid., 469.
12. Ibid.
13. Rawls, *A Theory of Justice,* 383. More generally, for Rawls's discussion of obedience and disobedience to unjust laws, see 350–355, 363–391.

Objections and Replies

THIS BOOK BEGAN WITH A PRACTICAL QUESTION OF POLITICAL philosophy: What overall attitude should you or I have toward governments and the laws governments impose on us? In attempting to answer this question, we have looked at four different views: super patriotism, political cynicism, anarchism, and critical citizenship. Of these, the critical citizenship view appears to provide the best answer to questions about government legitimacy and the duty to obey the law.

Like every philosophy, however, the critical citizenship view can generate further questions and objections. While I cannot anticipate all of these, in this chapter, I will try to clarify and strengthen the critical citizenship view by raising some questions and some objections to the view.

> *Question: Suppose that a person adopts the critical citizenship view. What does this view have to say about the many controversial issues people face in contemporary society? Is it any help in trying to decide about issues like abortion, the death penalty, affirmative action, flag burning, or censorship?*

The most direct answer to this question is no. The critical citizenship view has nothing specific to say about most controversial issues. The reason for this is that the view is designed to answer certain general questions about the moral status of laws and governments, but it is not meant to provide a complete ideology or decision-making principle. It tells us to apply rational and moral standards to governments, laws, and policies, but it does not tell us what to think about specific ones.

This is not a weakness of the view, because in any specific controversy there are many different kinds of issues to consider. In addition, factual information about the probable results of adopting one policy rather than another is always relevant, and no general philosophical outlook can provide this. To take an example, if one wants to reach a reasonable view about the legitimacy of a practice like the death penalty, then it is important to answer a variety of questions about the death penalty. For example, does the death penalty protect innocent lives by deterring murders? Or does it jeopardize innocent lives by making it possible for people to be executed for crimes they did not commit? If it does deter murders, does it do this more effectively than other lesser punishments? Can the death penalty be applied in a fair and consistent manner? Is it a "cruel and unusual punishment"? These are among the questions critical citizens should raise in considering this problem, but the critical citizenship view by itself cannot answer them.[1]

Adopting this view, then, represents a beginning point for reflection on many questions rather than an end point. In fact, one of the key elements of the critical citizenship view is its emphasis on the legitimacy of questioning and criticizing governmental laws and policies. Given the lack of a guarantee that governments, laws, and policies are good, the critical citizenship view rejects the ideal of unquestioning acceptance and opposes efforts to stifle political criticism. For this reason, critical citizens are likely to be suspicious of censorship and attempts to limit political criticism. Even in this case, however, critical citizens need not be opposed to every form of censorship. In general, because the critical citizenship view does not imply a specific stance on most issues, people who hold this view may disagree with one another when other political issues arise.

Question: Isn't the critical citizenship view really the same as anarchism? Both views allow a person to go along with laws that he or she agrees with, and both approve of disobedience when a person believes the law is wrong. Isn't critical citizenship just anarchism in disguise?

Critical citizenship shares with anarchism a stress on the importance of individual judgment and autonomy. Both agree that it may be morally right to disobey the law some of the time.

Nonetheless, the two views are different in important ways. While anarchists do not acknowledge any obligation to obey the law *because* it is the law, critical citizens do. When laws grow out of governments and processes that are worthy of respect, then critical citizens will acknowledge that they are generally obligated to obey them. Moreover, they may be obligated even in cases where they disagree with a law and think it is a bad one. If a good and fair procedure gives rise to a law that is inefficient or creates minor injustices, then critical citizens will feel obligated to obey in spite of their disapproval of the specific law. It is only when the law is seriously unjust or immoral that disobedience could be legitimate.

So from the critical citizenship point of view, if the government and the lawmaking procedures are worthy of respect, then there is a strong presumption in favor of obeying the laws they create. For anarchists, there is never any presumption in favor of obedience, no matter how good the government is, and saying "It's the law" never adds any weight to an argument, while it does count for critical citizens.

In addition, while it is hard to imagine that an anarchist could be patriotic, critical citizens may well be patriots. They may identify with their country and value its institutions. They may take pride in the processes that give rise to laws or the protections that laws and governments provide for citizens. These positive attitudes are compatible with critical citizenship in a way that they are not with anarchism.[2]

Question: If the critical citizenship view is not a form of anarchism, then isn't it just the view that civil disobedience is sometimes justified? Is that all it comes to?

The claim that disobeying the law may sometimes be morally justified is central to the critical citizenship view and is of obvious importance to people like Thoreau, King, and Gandhi who defend civil disobedience. While the two views are linked in this way, they are not identical. The critical citizenship view goes far beyond merely affirming that civil disobedience is sometimes morally right.

In order to see why this is so, we need to define the term *civil disobedience* more precisely. To commit civil disobedience, one must violate a law, but not every act of violating a law is an act of civil disobedience. When people commit civil disobedience, they violate the law in a manner that is public and nonviolent, and their violation is motivated by a desire to protest against a government law or policy. All three of these elements—being public, being nonviolent, and being motivated by the desire to protest—are necessary if an illegal act is to qualify as civil disobedience.[3]

Suppose that three different people reach the conclusion that it is immoral to pay taxes to support the construction of nuclear weapons. Person A evades his taxes by not reporting his income to the government. Person B publicly announces that she will pay no taxes. Person C places a bomb in an Internal Revenue Service office. All three people are protesting against a government policy, but only B commits civil disobedience because only B's act is public and nonviolent. Because A keeps his act secret and C's act is violent, neither constitutes civil disobedience. Likewise, if person D simply cheats on his income tax in order to keep the money for himself, he is not committing civil disobedience because his act is not public and is not motivated by a desire to protest against a law or policy. Civil disobedience, then, is a very specific form of illegal action.

While the critical citizenship view does agree that this form of action *may* be justified, this is not all the critical citizenship view amounts to. Remember that the critical citizenship view says that in determining whether we have an obligation to obey the law, we need to consider the nature of the government as a whole, the nature of the procedures by which laws and policies are made, and the nature of the laws themselves. If a government is bad enough, then there is no obligation to obey its laws at all. Therefore, any acts of disobedience—as long as they were not immoral on other grounds—would be justified. The disobedience need not be public, need not be nonviolent, and need not be done in protest to be justified. In short, it need not be an act of civil disobedience. So from the critical citizenship perspective, acts of civil disobedience are simply *one* form of potentially justified violations of laws. While advocates of civil disobedience seek to justify a very narrow and limited set of illegal actions, the critical citizenship view does not say that this is the only form of illegal action that is justified.

However, just as critical citizenship looks critically at obedience to law, it looks equally carefully at disobedience. No form of disobedience is automatically justified. Even public, nonviolent protests may be immoral if the laws they are protesting are justified and legitimate. Just as the obligation to obey depends on facts about governments and laws, so too the rightness of disobeying depends on similar facts. Disobedience to just laws and governments is as unjustified as obedience to unjust laws and governments.

The key point here is that the critical citizenship view is more general in scope than a mere commitment to civil disobedience. The critical citizenship view is compatible with much that defenders of civil disobedience say, and, indeed, it might be viewed as the more general view that is implicit in defenses of civil disobedience. Nonetheless, the issue of civil disobedience is just one aspect of the broader set of questions that the critical citizenship view seeks to answer.

> *A Hobbesian objection: You accept Hobbes's view that government may be necessary to provide security to people, but you ignore his argument that people must obey the law and not put the judgment of their conscience above the law. Aren't you overlooking the importance of unquestioning obedience for ensuring the ability of governments to keep the peace?*

This objection stresses an accurate point about Hobbes. In writing *Leviathan,* Hobbes was not simply arguing that there should be some form of government or other. He was arguing for the more specific conclusion that there should be an authoritarian government, a government with virtually unlimited powers to do whatever it thought necessary to keep the peace.

Hobbes further believed that dissent by individuals would simply undermine the government, and he thought the government had a right to control the views people could express. He wanted to limit the right to criticize because he feared that dissent would diminish the power of the government. And once this happened, he thought, then people would ignore the government and sink back into a war of all against all. For Hobbes, the only thing that can hold people in check is a sovereign power that is absolute in its ability to determine what laws are necessary and in its power to enforce these laws vigorously.

As he wrote, "[I]t belongeth of right, to whatsoever man or assembly that hath the sovereignty, to be judge . . . of the means of peace and defense . . . and to do whatsoever he shall think necessary . . . for the preservation of peace and security. . . . "[4]

So, Hobbes would not have approved of the critical citizenship view and its recognition of an individual right to violate seriously unjust laws. Indeed, he went so far as to claim that nothing that the sovereign (the governing power) did could be unjust because the sovereign had a right to do anything necessary to preserving the peace.[5]

The fact that Hobbes thought that only an authoritarian government could keep the peace does not mean that he was correct about this. There are in fact good reasons for accepting Hobbes's view that there ought to be a government, while rejecting his claim that governments ought to have unlimited powers and should always be obeyed. Hobbes is simply not convincing when he argues that governments cannot possibly be unjust and should be unrestricted in their powers. Either he overlooks or underestimates the possibility that life under a bad government could actually be worse than life in the state of nature.

For this reason, he overlooks the possibility that a weaker government might actually provide more security for people than a government that is totally unchecked in its powers. History testifies to the terrible abuses that governments themselves are capable of and provides evidence for the need for citizens to act in ways that challenge and limit government powers.

Finally, even Hobbes admits that people sometimes have a right to disobey. He argues that because people sign the social contract and set up a government in order to protect themselves from injury and death, they retain a right to protect themselves from injury or death at the hands of the state. As he wrote, "If the sovereign command a man, though justly condemned, to kill, wound, or maim himself; or not to resist those that assault him . . . yet hath that man the liberty to disobey."[6]

What this passage shows is that for all his emphasis on the absolute obligation to obey the law, Hobbes actually concedes that disobedience may be justified, and that, of course, is what the critical citizenship view emphasizes.

A cynic's objection: You've just pointed out that governments are extremely dangerous institutions. What you omit, however, is that the whole function of government is to serve the interests of some favored subgroup within society. They do not exist to serve the public good. Maybe this is not necessarily true, but it is so much the usual situation that we can assume it. The probability that any existing government really deserves our respect is so low that it is foolish to take seriously the obligation to obey the law. On this point, anarchists are absolutely correct and critical citizens are naive and mistaken.

Cynics appreciate just the things that Hobbes overlooked. Hobbes was so worried about the evils of anarchy that he underplayed the evils of government. This is understandable. He lived in a time of civil war and experienced the insecurity of a situation in which there was no single, unchallenged sovereign power. Perhaps, at the time, any government would have been an improvement. Nonetheless, it does not follow that that is always the case.

What cynics overlook is that it may be possible to control government officials, to prevent abuse of power, and thus to make government the servant rather than the master of people. While cynics may be right that it is almost inevitable that the powers held by government officials will be abused, it does not follow that nothing can be done about this problem. In fact, both political theorists and practical reformers have devoted a great deal of thought and effort to what we might call the problem of preventing tyranny. And if one were able to create a nontyrannical government that actually served the public good, then it might well be worthy of our respect and support.

How is it possible, then, to limit and contain the tendency toward tyranny? This is too big a question to answer fully, but I will mention a few famous attempts to deal with it. In *The Republic,* Plato proposes that we prevent tyranny by carefully educating and testing those who will govern. He claims that if potential rulers are properly educated and are then subjected to tests of character, then those who qualify will be virtuous and incorruptible. They will desire the well-being of the state rather than personal happiness and so will not abuse their powers for personal gain. Anyone who fails to possess the right traits will not be permitted to serve in government.[7]

John Locke pursues a different strategy to prevent tyranny in his *Second Treatise on Civil Government.* Unlike Plato, he does not focus on the moral or psychological traits of the rulers. Rather, he tries to design the institutions of government so as to prevent tyranny even if the wrong type of person comes to power. Locke makes a number of proposals. First, he proposes that the various powers of government be separated so that no one person or branch has too much unchecked authority. According to his "separation of powers" model, the king has the authority to enforce the laws, but the laws themselves are made by a separate legislative branch of government. Moreover, since it is kings (or, more generally, those in the executive branch of government) who tend toward tyranny, Locke wants the elected legislature to possess the ultimate political authority. In addition, there are specific rules that the king himself must obey. For example, the king must not prevent the legislature from meeting.

Second, Locke provides a criterion for judging what constitutes abuse of power. He does this by stressing the existence of individual rights. According to Locke, individuals have natural rights to life, liberty, and property. These rights exist independently of the government, and the government has no authority to act in ways that violate these rights.

Finally, Locke argues that if these individual rights are violated or if the king violates other conditions of his holding power, then the people have a right to overthrow the king and deprive him of his power.

Central themes in Locke's view can be seen, then, as suggestions for how to ensure that governments work for the public good rather than for the good of the rulers themselves. Separation of governmental powers, recognition of individual rights, and the right to revolution are all means for controlling government and preventing the development of tyranny.

These proposals by Plato and Locke are just two examples of the many strategies political theorists have devised to prevent tyranny. Another important idea is the requirement that officials be limited to specific terms of office and that they be popularly elected in order to hold office. Elections give citizens some control over who holds political power in a society and make it clear that no one holds such power unconditionally. In addition, elections force rulers who want to stay in office to attend to the needs and interests of the voters. If voting rights are widely distributed, then, at least in theory, the rulers must attend to the needs and interests of most people. Regular elections give citizens a way of changing leaders without violence and without waiting for the situation to become intolerable.

The key point about these proposals is that they acknowledge and seek to answer the cynic's claims about the potential evils that government may do. Advocates of these proposals recognize the temptations of power, but they believe that it is possible to design governments in a way that prevents (or significantly limits) these abuses.

To the extent that they succeed, then a government may actually function in the public interest and may be worthy of support. There is, of course, no guarantee that this will occur. Nonetheless, it may be possible to design institutions in ways that make it more difficult for government officials to use their power solely on behalf of some influential subgroup.

The cynic's insight about the actual and possible evils of government needs to be seen as the first word, not the last word about government. It makes clear the challenge that faces those who want nontyrannical governments, and provides additional support for the critical citizen's insistence that obedience to laws must be conditional on the nature of the laws and governments involved.

> *A Socratic objection: The problem with the critical citizenship view is that it puts too much stress on individual agreement with particular laws. Socrates correctly saw that consent is merely one of the bases of political obligation. He denied that it was the only one and rightly held that there are obligations that we do not freely choose. In contrast, critical citizens seem to think that people only have the obligations they choose to have. This is false.*

This objection rests on a misunderstanding of the critical citizenship view. Nonetheless, it contains an important challenge to the idea that the only obligations we have are ones that we consent to. While I criticized Socrates' parent argument and benefactor argument in Chapter 2, I do not fully reject the points made in this objection. I believe, however, that the critical citizenship view is compatible with a belief in obligations that we do not consent to.

The question of consent to laws and governments is an issue of central importance. Consent is stressed in social contract theories and in historical documents like the Declaration of Independence, which tells us that governments derive their "just powers" (i.e., the ones that they legitimately possess) from the "consent of the governed." This implies that if a power is not consented to, then it is unjustly held.

How should we interpret the requirement that governments must be consented to in order to be just? If we take this to mean that a government or law is legitimate only if every person under its jurisdiction consents to it, then we are led to the kind of anarchist view defended by Robert Paul Wolff.[8] This is not an interpretation that would be supported by critical citizens, however, since they reject anarchism.

Even those of us who are not anarchists, however, are probably attracted to the idea that the "consent of the governed" is necessary for legitimacy. We need, therefore, to clarify the basis of the claim that a person may have obligations to obey a law, even though that person has not and would not consent to the law. How can this idea be supported? The easiest way is to imagine some law that seems highly justified and to imagine someone who would not consent to it. Imagine, for example, someone who wants to kill people he doesn't like. This person might not be willing to consent to a law that forbids murder. If he claims, however, that the government has no legitimate authority to enforce laws that forbid murder against him because he never consented to these laws, I doubt that many would accept his argument. Virtually everyone views murder as a serious crime and an immoral action. We believe that laws against murder are justified, and we do not think that people have no obligation to obey these laws just because they did not consent to them. If this is so, then obligations to obey specific laws can exist in the absence of consent to them.

Critical citizens judge the obligation to obey on the basis of the nature of the government, the lawmaking procedures, and the content of the law. A law can be a good one and can be binding even on people who do not consent to it. Consent is not an absolute requirement for the legitimacy of a law.

Similarly, Socrates is correct that a government may be legitimate, even if it has not been consented to by every citizen. Nonetheless, his own arguments for this view are flawed. As I argued earlier, Socrates is incorrect in his view that being born in a place is sufficient for generating an obligation to obey the laws of that place. He is mistaken because a person who is born in a society but is mistreated by it is not obligated to support it. The extreme example of such a person is a slave, but other forms of mistreatment would also undermine obligations.

Socrates is also mistaken that receiving benefits from a society gives rise to an obligation to obey its laws. A person who receives benefits from a society is not obligated to support it if the society as a whole is unjust. A member of a privileged elite whose comfortable position derives from the unjust treatment of others is not morally obligated to support the laws and policies of her country. If anything, receiving benefits that derive from the unjust treatment of others may impose an obligation to seek change and to disobey.

Thoreau expresses this point very effectively. After denying that a person has a duty "to devote himself to the eradication of any, even the most enormous wrongs," he goes on to affirm that "it is his duty, at least, to wash his hands of it, and . . . not to give it practically his support." Bringing the conclusion to a personal level, he goes on to say, "If I devote myself to other pursuits and contemplations, I must first see, at least, that I do not pursue them sitting upon another man's shoulders. I must get off him first, that he may pursue his contemplations too."[9] From his point of view, then, one has a duty not to support regimes from which one benefits if one's benefits are enjoyed at the expense of others.

Socrates' appeals to birth and to benefits are not sufficient, then, to generate obligations. If, however, one is born into a system and benefits from it and if the system dispenses benefits in a manner that is generally just, then one is obligated to support it, whether or not one has consented or would consent to it. Socrates is right that obligations to a society can exist in the absence of consent and agreement, but he fails to see that such obligations exist only if the system treats both one-self and others in a way that is fitting and fair.

In other words, whether they have consented or not, people have a duty to support institutions that are just and fair. They do not have a duty to support unjust institutions, however. Of course, in the real world, no government or society is perfectly just, and so we have to make judgments about the extent to which a particular government approximates ideals of justice and deserves our support. As John Rawls writes, "if the basic structure of society is just, or as just as it is reasonable to expect in the circumstances, everyone has a natural duty to do his part in the existing scheme. Each is bound to these institutions independent of his voluntary acts. . . . "[10]

The Socratic objection, then, is mistaken both in its assumptions about the critical citizenship view and in its understanding of the basis for obligations that people have not consented to. Individual obligations are acquired not simply by agreement, by birth, or by benefit. They arise as a result of the justice or injustice of the institutions under which a person lives.

> *A libertarian objection: One view that you've neglected is libertarianism. Libertarians agree that governments are necessary to protect people from violent assault, and they would support a government that limited itself to legitimate protective functions. Unfortunately, they say, all modern states go beyond this, forcing citizens to pay taxes to support welfare programs and other kinds of public assistance. Libertarians reject the idea that governments may tax us in order to benefit other people. Such governments violate our rights and are thus illegitimate. For this reason, they say, we have no moral obligation to support them.*

While cynics criticize governments for serving the interests of the governing elite, libertarians criticize governments for serving the interests of needy, nonelite groups. Libertarians believe that the only legitimate state is the "minimal" or "night watchman" state, a government that is, in Robert Nozick's words, "limited to the functions of protecting all its citizens against violence, theft, fraud, and to the enforcement of contracts."[11] Libertarians are strong believers in the existence and importance of individual rights, and they denounce more extensive government activities as violations of their rights.

What is the relation between libertarianism and the critical citizenship view? In principle, there is no conflict between them. A critical citizen could be a libertarian, judging that welfare states are tyrannical and rejecting obligations to them. There is, however, no necessity that critical citizens embrace the libertarian view or see welfare state activities (such as providing education, housing, health care, or job training to people) as illegitimate. Moreover, there are good reasons, I think, why people ought to reject the libertarian view. While libertarians are correct to be concerned about guarding individual rights from government power, I believe that they are mistaken in thinking that using tax money to help persons in need violates individual rights.

One defender of libertarianism, Robert Nozick, argues that "welfare state" activities violate people's rights by forcing them to pay taxes for activities that they may not approve. In supporting his view, Nozick makes it clear that he has no objection to voluntary acts of charity, but rejects forced assistance, claiming that "taxation of earnings from labor is on a par with forced labor." He then asks the following rhetorical question: "[I]f it would be illegitimate for a tax system to seize some of a man's leisure (forced labor) for the purpose of serving the needy, how can it be legitimate for a tax system to seize some of a man's goods for that purpose?"[12] While Nozick does not answer this question explicitly, he clearly believes that it is not legitimate. For him, both forced labor and forced contributions are immoral practices that violate people's moral rights.

It is important to consider this objection in a discussion of citizenship because questions about levels of taxation and about how much individuals owe to society at large are matters of great controversy. In the United States, many citizens believe that tax levels are too high and that individuals should have more control over the money they earn. Since paying taxes is one of the central duties of citizenship, it is important to determine whether taxes are legitimate and whether certain common activities of governments are in fact illegitimate abuses of their power.

If we examine the passage quoted from Nozick, there appear to be two separate arguments that he might be putting forth. He might be arguing that all taxation (forced contribution of money) violates people's rights and is, therefore, inherently immoral. Or he might be arguing that while taxation can be legitimate for some purposes, there is something special about "the purpose of serving the needy" (or other activities that go beyond minimal state functions) that makes taxation for this purpose illegitimate.

Let's consider the first argument. Nozick's claim that taxation is "on a par with forced labor" strongly suggests that all taxation is inherently unjust. This is because we tend to think that forced labor is a horrible and unjust practice. The phrase "forced labor" itself calls up frightening images of people in chains, people who lack liberty and are suffering hardship. So if forced labor is unjust and if taxation is morally on a par with forced labor, then taxation is unjust.

In thinking about this argument, it is important to remember that no government can function without taxes of some form. Every government requires resources to carry out its functions. Even a minimal state of the sort that libertarians favor needs money to support armies, police forces, courts, and other agencies to enforce contracts. Because they favor some form of government, then, libertarians must support the use of tax money to pay for the functions it carries out. In fact, Nozick himself explicitly argues that it is legitimate to require people to pay to provide these services to all citizens.[13] So it is misleading to suggest, as his "forced labor" argument does, that taxation is necessarily unjust. This cannot be the argument he is relying on, because it is inconsistent with his approval of the minimal state.

To put this another way, since Nozick approves of some taxation, he must either retract his claim that all taxation is morally "on a par with forced labor," or he must agree that forced labor is sometimes morally justified. If he holds that forced labor is always immoral and that all taxation is morally equivalent to forced labor, then he cannot consistently support taxation for minimal state activities. Since he does support this kind of taxation, he cannot consistently hold the views required for the "forced labor" argument.

If Nozick were to object to *all* taxation because it is coercive, he would in effect be adopting the anarchist view. If the only people who pay money to support "state" activities do so voluntarily, then one does not have a real state. One has the kind of voluntary association that anarchists favor. If one criticizes taxation because one thinks that coercion is always wrong, then one is committed to anarchism because, as we have seen earlier, all law is inherently coercive. Laws require people to act in certain ways whether they want to or not and threaten them with punishment if they fail to do so. So to condemn taxation because it is coercive is to assume the anarchist view that people should only have to do what they voluntarily choose to do.

Libertarians, however, are not anarchists. Therefore, they must believe that some coercion is legitimate. Further, if carrying out the tasks of the minimal state requires taxation, then libertarians must think that taxation can be legitimate.

If taxation can be legitimate, then we need to ask why libertarians think taxation is legitimate when it is used to provide police protection but is illegitimate when it is used to provide health care, housing, or other "welfare" services. Why is it that taxation providing police protection to those who need it is a legitimate government activity but taxation providing health, housing, or education to those who need it is "on a par with forced labor"?

While libertarians do have arguments for their view, I do not think that they can answer this question satisfactorily.[14] They cannot show that the activities of the modern welfare state are illegitimate. In order to see why, let us return to the kind of reasoning Hobbes used to justify the existence of the state. Hobbes showed that in the state of nature, people would lack the means to protect themselves effectively from violence and assault by other people. They would agree to form a government in order to provide protection against attack from others.

Suppose we ask why people want protection from violent attack. It could be that there is something especially terrible about violent attack, or it could be that people want to be safe and secure and that violent attack is one form of threat to their security. Hobbes thought it is security that people want. People do not want to die or suffer injury or pain. So they seek to prevent violent attacks against themselves because these are causes of death, injury, and pain. This is a plausible view.

We know, however, that violent attack is not the only cause of harm to people. People can be killed and injured by natural phenomena like floods, fires, famine, and disease, just as they can be harmed by the violent acts of other people. So if people can be seriously harmed by natural events and if they can obtain protection against these natural threats by using government institutions, it seems as rational to use government for these functions as it is to use government to protect us from violent attacks. There is no reason to draw a line and say that government activity to prevent violent attack is legitimate but government activity to prevent harm from natural disasters is illegitimate.

Violent attack and natural disasters are not the only threats to people's well-being, however. In addition, people can be seriously harmed by social and economic phenomena over which they have no control. Inflation, depression, unemployment, environmental pollution, inadequate housing, inadequate medical care, lack of education, and technological change can seriously harm people and are significant sources of insecurity. The harms caused by these social phenomena are as serious as the harms caused by violence and by natural disasters. Since what people want is security and a decent life, it is just as rational to sign a social contract that sets up a government to protect people from natural and social evils as it is to sign a contract that sets up a government to protect people from violent assault. There is no reason why people should limit the functions of a government to a "minimal state" that protects against violent attack but offers no protection against other kinds of threats.

Finally, if it is as legitimate for governments to provide these kinds of protective services as it is for governments to provide police protection and other "minimal state" functions, then it follows that the use of tax money for these "welfare state" activities can be as legitimate as the use of tax money for "minimal state" activities. If it is permissible to coerce people to provide tax money for police services (as Nozick and other libertarians concede), then it is hard to see why it violates people's rights to require them to pay taxes for government agencies that protect people against natural and social sources of harm and insecurity.

So, if we return to the logic of Hobbes's argument for government, we can see that the argument provides a justification both for "minimal state" activities and for "welfare state" activities. In addition, the Hobbesian type of argument is not the only one we can appeal to. We can justify the legitimacy of many government activities by appeal both to self-interest and to concern for other people. "Welfare state" functions of government serve our self-interest by providing a kind of insurance against harms to which virtually everyone is susceptible. Even if we are well off now, it is rational to want protections for ourselves if we should be harmed by natural or social changes. Likewise, if we care about other people

121

(including those who are strangers to us), we will be pleased to have institutions that protect them against the same evils that we personally hope to avoid. There is nothing about the critical citizenship view that requires us to reject these institutions.

> *A final objection: The term* critical citizenship *sounds awfully negative. It suggests a negative type of person who is always looking for what is wrong with governments. Shouldn't a reasonable political philosophy at least allow for and even encourage a more positive attitude toward politics and the duties of citizenship?*

It is true that words like *critical, critic,* and *criticism* have a somewhat negative sound to them. Critics are, we think, always looking for and often finding what's wrong with things. We think of critical people as people who fail to notice and appreciate what is good. For this reason, the image that may be suggested of the critical citizen is that of a chronic complainer, a person who is never satisfied with things.

I do not deny that the word *critical* has these connotations. But there are other meanings of a more positive sort that need to be kept in mind as well. Critical citizens are people who are mentally alert. They notice and think about things. They require good reasons for government policies and laws, and they think about the reasons that are offered to justify both actual and proposed laws and policies. For critical citizens, governments and laws are too important to allow us to support them uncritically. Only after it is clear that a government, law, or policy is actually a good one will critical citizens give their support to it. Only if it deserves support will it be supported. But if it is deserving, then critical citizens can give it their enthusiastic and wholehearted support.

To find the term *critical citizenship* a negative one is to overlook two things. First, it overlooks the positive aspects of being critical that I have mentioned—mental alertness, a concern for justification, a sense of the importance of government decisions and policies. Second, it overlooks the presence of the word *citizenship*. Unlike anarchists or extreme cynics, critical citizens take their role as citizens seriously. Knowing what they know about governments, they may be wary of the negative potential of government, but they also take seriously their own membership in political society. While some critical citizens may want to do the absolute minimum required by citizenship, others may feel strongly about doing their fair share to help bring about a just society. Exactly how to do this will depend on the particular political system and society to which one belongs and on one's own special abilities. While there is no single way for all individuals to promote justice in their societies, critical citizens may be as positively committed to this task as anyone else.

A Final Note to the Reader

I began this book with the question, how should we think and feel about government institutions? In pursuing this question, I have examined several different views and have tried to show that the philosophy of critical citizenship provides the best overall answer to this question.

While I have worked hard to support this view and to show why other views are less successful in answering my initial question, my discussion remains incomplete in a number of ways. I would like to acknowledge this incompleteness by raising some questions that I think readers of this book ought to think about.

The first question is for readers who remain unconvinced that the critical citizenship view is correct. You may hold some other view, one of the views discussed in the book or another that I have overlooked. If you favor a view that I have rejected, then look at the arguments I gave against the view and try to show where my arguments go wrong. Did I misinterpret the view? Or did I take an invalid objection to be decisive? Likewise, compare your view with the others considered in this book. How well does it deal with the issues that have been discussed?

If you accept the critical citizenship view, then you are still faced with some important and difficult problems. The critical citizenship view makes our obligations as citizens partly dependent on the justice and injustice of the institutions under which we live. You need to ask yourself what it takes for a government to be just and whether your own government measures up to standards of justice. In turn, this will lead you to questions about what the standards of justice are, to questions about what the government you live under stands for, and questions about what it actually does. In addition, you need to look at important laws and policies to see if they satisfy the requirements of justice and morality. Answering these questions is not always easy.

Finally, when you arrive at answers to these questions, you will have to decide what to do with your answers. What do your answers imply about your own activities and way of life? What degree of political or social activity should you engage in? Is concern with political activity and social issues something that you can either take or leave, depending on your tastes and interests? Or is this something that you are morally bound to incorporate into your life? What arguments could you give to defend either choice, whether it is concern or noninvolvement?

And if you think you do have some duty to improve things, what is the scope of this duty? Should you be concerned only about the well-being of people you know and personally care about? Or about people throughout your own country? Or about people throughout the world? And however you answer these questions, how much of your life should be devoted to issues of justice, peace, and human well-being? Is it enough to make small contributions of time, energy, or money? Or is some greater degree of concern and commitment required in order for you to do your fair share?

In short, whether you agree or disagree with my overall view in this book, I want to leave you with a challenge to further thought. If you disagree with my views and arguments, then I challenge you to figure out why you disagree and to do a better job defending your own view than you think I have done in defending mine. If you are a reader who agrees with the philosophy of critical citizenship, then I challenge you to figure out what specific political views and attitudes are appropriate to you and how these should be expressed in the way you live your life.

Notes

1. For my attempt to answer questions regarding the legitimacy of using death as a form of punishment, see Stephen Nathanson, *An Eye for an Eye?—The Morality of Punishing by Death* (Totowa, NJ: Rowman and Littlefield, 1987).
2. For a discussion of the compatibility of patriotism and a critical attitude, see Stephen Nathanson, "In Defense of 'Moderate Patriotism,'" *Ethics* 99 (1989), 535–552.
3. On defining civil disobedience, see Hugo Bedau, "On Civil Disobedience," *Journal of Philosophy* 58 (1961), 653–661.
4. Hobbes, *Leviathan*, chap. 18.
5. Ibid.
6. Ibid., chap. 21.
7. See Plato, *The Republic of Plato*, Book 3, 412B–Book 4, 421C.
8. For a particularly clear statement of Wolff's consent requirement, see his "Afterword," in *The Rule of Law*, ed. R. P. Wolff (New York: Simon & Schuster, 1971), especially 248–251.
9. Thoreau, "Civil Disobedience," 287–288.
10. Rawls, *A Theory of Justice*, 115.
11. Nozick, *Anarchy, State, and Utopia*, 26.
12. Ibid., 169, 170.
13. See ibid., 26–27.
14. Nozick's book contains many arguments that I cannot consider here. A similar view is defended by Milton Friedman in *Capitalism and Freedom* (Chicago: University of Chicago Press, 1962), chaps. 10–12.

The purpose of this brief listing is to provide some advice for readers who want to further explore problems about political obligation and about political philosophy more generally. It includes books that are not already cited in the bibliography.

For a broader acquaintance with issues in political philosophy, one might want to start either with a general survey of the field or a collection of classic writings. For a general survey, see N. Bowie and R. Simon, *The Individual and the Political Order* (Englewood Cliffs, NJ: Prentice-Hall, 1977). A useful anthology of classic readings is J. Somerville and R. Santoni, eds., *Social and Political Philosophy* (Garden City, NY: Doubleday [Anchor Books], 1963). An anthology that combines classical and contemporary writings is R. Garner and A. Oldenquist, eds., *Society and the Individual: Readings in Political and Social Philosophy* (Belmont, CA: Wadsworth, 1990). For a collection that focuses on various aspects of the law, see J. Feinberg and H. Gross, eds., *Philosophy of Law* (Belmont, CA: Wadsworth, 1990).

Socrates' views on politics are presented by Plato in the *Apology* and the *Crito*. There are many editions of both. For discussion of Socrates' views, see A. D. Woozley, "Socrates on Disobeying the Law," in *The Philosophy of Socrates* (Notre Dame, IN: Notre Dame University Press, 1980) ed. G. Vlastos, 299–319, and Richard Kraut, *Socrates and the State* (Princeton, NJ: Princeton University Press, 1984).

Cynicism is not usually elaborated as a separate theoretical position. As I note in the text, Marxism incorporates a version of political cynicism. For selections of Marxist works, see Robert Tucker, ed., *The Marx-Engels Reader* (New York: Norton, 1972) or Eugene Kamenka, ed., *The Portable Karl Marx* (New York: Viking Penguin, 1983).

For anarchism, in addition to the works by Kropotkin, Tolstoy, and Wolff that are cited in the text, there is a good collection of anarchist writings in L. Krimerman and L. Perry, eds., *Patterns of Anarchy* (Garden City, NY: Doubleday [Anchor Books], 1966). For a general survey, see George Woodcock, *Anarchism: A History of Libertarian Ideas and Movements* (Cleveland, OH: Meridian, 1962). For a briefer account, see April Carter, *The Political Theory of Anarchism* (New York: Harper & Row, 1971). Jeffrey Reiman's *In Defense of Political Philosophy* (New York: Harper & Row, 1972) is a book-length reply to Wolff's *In Defense of Anarchy*.

Martin Luther King's views are expressed in a number of essays in the volume *Why We Can't Wait* (New York: New American Library, 1964). A variety of views about civil disobedience can be found in H. Bedau, ed., *Civil Disobedience: Theory and Practice* (New York: Pegasus, 1969), and in J. R. Pennock and J. Chapman, eds., *Nomos XII: Political and Legal Obligation* (Chicago: Aldine–Atherton, 1970). For two book-length discussions, see Peter Singer, *Democracy and Disobedience* (New York: Oxford, 1974), and Howard Zinn, *Disobedience and Democracy: Nine Fallacies on Law and Order* (New York: Vintage, 1968). I discuss some of the difficulties of evaluating nations in "On Deciding Whether a Nation Deserves Our Loyalty," *Public Affairs Quarterly* 4 (1990), 287–298.

For thoughtful discussions of citizenship and the role of criticism in politics, see the following works by Michael Walzer: *Obligations: Essays on Disobedience, War and Citizenship* (Cambridge, MA: Harvard University Press, 1970); *Interpretation and Social Criticism* (Cambridge, MA:

Harvard University Press, 1987); and *The Company of Critics* (New York: Basic Books, 1988).

On libertarianism, see the works by Robert Nozick and Milton Friedman cited in the text, as well as T. Machan, ed., *The Libertarian Reader* (Totowa, NJ: Rowman and Littlefield, 1982).

BIBLIOGRAPHY

Axelrod, Robert. *The Evolution of Cooperation.* New York: Basic Books, 1984.

Bedau, Hugo. "On Civil Disobedience." *Journal of Philosophy* 58 (1967), 653–661.

Dahl, Robert. *After the Revolution?—Authority in a Good Society.* New Haven, CT: Yale University Press, 1971.

———. *Democracy and Its Critics.* New Haven, CT: Yale University Press, 1990.

Fortas, Abe. *Concerning Dissent and Civil Disobedience.* New York: New American Library, 1968.

Friedman, David. *The Machinery of Freedom.* New York: Harper & Row, 1973.

Friedman, Milton. *Capitalism and Freedom.* Chicago: University of Chicago Press, 1962.

Gandhi, M. K. *Non-Violent Resistance.* New York: Schocken Books, 1961.

Garrison, William Lloyd. "Declaration of Sentiments, 1838." In S. Lynd, ed. *Nonviolence in America: A Documentary History.* Indianapolis: Bobbs-Merrill, 1966.

Golding, Martin. *Philosophy of Law.* Englewood Cliffs, NJ: Prentice-Hall, 1975.

Hobbes, Thomas. *Leviathan.* New York: Dutton Everyman Edition, 1950.

Kant, Immanuel. *Grounding for the Metaphysics of Morals.* (J. Ellington, trans.). Indianapolis: Hackett, 1981.

King, M. L., Jr. "Letter from Birmingham City Jail." In S. Lynd, ed., *Nonviolence in America: A Documentary History.* Indianapolis: Bobbs-Merrill, 1966.

Kropotkin, Peter. *Kropotkin's Revolutionary Pamphlets.* (Roger Baldwin, ed.). New York: Dover, 1970.

Lenin, V. I. "State and Revolution." In J. Somerville and R. Santoni, eds., *Social and Political Philosophy.* Garden City, NY: Doubleday (Anchor Books), 1963.

Lynd, S., ed. *Nonviolence in America: A Documentary History.* Indianapolis: Bobbs-Merrill, 1966.

Locke, John. *Two Treatises on Civil Government.*

Murphy, J., and J. Coleman. *The Philosophy of Law.* Totowa, NJ: Rowman and Allanheld, 1984.

Narveson, Jan. "Pacifism: A Philosophical Analysis." *Ethics* 75 (1965), 259–271.

Nathanson, Stephen. *An Eye for an Eye?—The Morality of Punishing by Death.* Totowa, NJ: Rowman and Littlefield, 1987.

———. "In Defense of 'Moderate Patriotism.'" *Ethics* 99 (1989), 535–552.

Nozick, Robert. *Anarchy, State, and Utopia.* New York: Basic Books, 1973.

Plato. "Crito." In *The Dialogues of Plato,* vol. 1. (Benjamin Jowett, trans.). New York: Random House, 1937.

Plato. *The Republic of Plato.* (F. M. Cornford, trans.). New York: Oxford University Press, 1945.

Rawls, John. *A Theory of Justice.* Cambridge: Harvard University Press, 1971.

Rice, Les. "The Banks of Marble." In Pete Seeger and Bob Reiser, eds., *Carry It On!—A History in Song and Pictures of the Working Men and Women of America.* New York: Simon & Schuster, 1985.

Bibliography

Rousseau, J. J. *Discourse on the Origins of Inequality.*

Thoreau, Henry David. "Civil Disobedience." In B. Atkinson, ed. *Walden and Other Writings of Henry David Thoreau.* New York: Random House, Modern Library, 1937.

Tolstoy, Leo. *Tolstoy's Writings on Civil Disobedience and Nonviolence.* New York: New American Library, 1968.

Wolff, R. P. *In Defense of Anarchism.* New York: Harper & Row, 1970.

———, ed. *The Rule of Law.* New York: Simon & Schuster, 1971.

INDEX

Boldfaced numbers indicate main discussions.

State of nature, 70, 72–75, 79–80
Super patriotism, **10–12**, 14, 22,
 25–38, 53, 86–87, 91, 96–97,
 99–100

Taxation, 15–16, 117–121
Thoreau, Henry David, 60, 92,
 106, 115

Thrasymachus, 12–15, 18, 42, 44,
 46–47
Tyranny, prevention of, 110–113

War, 65
Welfare State, 117–122
Wolff, Robert Paul, 17, 42, 60–61,
 82, 86–87, 89, 91, 114